Don't Sprint the Marathon

V. Raghunathan's first career was as an academic – as Professor of Finance at IIM, Ahmedabad, for nearly two decades, until early 2001. His second – a corporate one – started in 2001, first as President, ING Vysya Bank for about four years, and then with the GMR Group – an infrastructure major. He is currently CEO, GMR Varalakshmi Foundation. Also, since 1990 he has been an Adjunct Professor at the University of Bocconi, Milan, lecturing on behavioural finance.

Raghu has published over 400 academic papers and popular articles, and six books. He is the author of the best-seller *Games Indians Play - Why We Are the Way We Are* (Penguin, 2006), and *Stock Exchanges, Investments and Derivatives* (Tata McGraw Hill, 2007). He also writes a regular guest column in *The Economic Times* and monthly pieces in *Mint* and is a busy public speaker.

He has probably the largest private collection of old locks in the country, has been a cartoonist with a national daily, has played chess at all-India level, and sketched competitively in the past.

His website is www.vraghunathan.com.

Contents

Author's note ix

1. Will this book help you? 1

2. If life is a race... 5

3. Sprint versus marathon 11

4. Child – the parent of man 21

5. Developing the right attitude to life 37

6. Can ordinary walkers jog? 61

7. Let children grow in their own time 71

8. Schooling, work life and competition 83

9. Get interested in reading – anything at all 96

10. Schooling for mediocrity 112

11. If you could mail-order your child 133

12. School them young? 140

13. Reaching out to children 147

14. The last word 161

Index 163

To Harsh, Prashant, and Sahil – young marathoners, the three of them!

First published in India in 2010 by
HarperCollins *Publishers* India
a joint venture with
The India Today Group

ISBN: 978-81-7223-857-5

2 4 6 8 10 9 7 5 3 1

HarperCollins *Publishers*
A-53, Sector 57, Noida 201301, India
77-85 Fulham Palace Road, London W6 8JB, United Kingdom
Hazelton Lanes, 55 Avenue Road, Suite 2900, Toronto, Ontario M5R 3L2
and 1995 Markham Road, Scarborough, Ontario M1B 5M8, Canada
25 Ryde Road, Pymble, Sydney, NSW 2073, Australia
31 View Road, Glenfield, Auckland 10, New Zealand
10 East 53rd Street, New York NY 10022, USA

Typeset in Adobe Caslon 11/14.5
InoSoft Systems

Printed and bound at
Thomson Press (India) Ltd.

DON'T SPRINT THE MARATHON

V. Raghunathan

HarperCollins *Publishers* India
a joint venture with

New Delhi

Author's note

WE REGULARLY COME ACROSS PARENTS WHO PUSH themselves and who push their children to their limits in a bid to make them superachievers. Their assumption seems to be, if their child did not make it to a top engineering, medical or management school, somehow that's a letdown. They would speak of their child with a little less pride if the child did not score 95 per cent in the CBSE finals or make it to a good engineering or medical college, or score a big SAT score and make it into an Ivy League college in the US. There are also those among us, who, unless they are in high-profile careers, somehow feel life has passed them by, and give up on all enthusiasm. Then there are those in high-profile careers who have little time for their near and dear, or for their hobbies and interests, till it is too late. I have had my share of friends and acquaintances in all the above categories – who hasn't?

Then there are all those reports that one sees in the newspapers regularly about children killing themselves, unable to bear the examination pressure. We see a number of schools where teaching is so routine that learning is given short shrift. It appears to me that a lot of parents, teachers and professionals are guilty of preparing their own lives and those of their children as if life were a sprint. The fact is that life is not a sprint at all. Rather, it mimics a marathon more. Clearly, much of today's generation has all the wrong coaches for the race they have to run!

It was to address these issues that I decided to write this book, aimed at parents, teachers and other adults – especially the overambitious ones.

In the course of writing this book, five remarkable 'marathoners' helped me with their time. These, in the alphabetical order of their surnames, are, Ela R. Bhatt, Ashwini Datta (formerly Ashwini Nachappa), N.R. Narayana Murthy, G.M. Rao, and Kallam Anji Reddy. I had sought their valuable time so that I could include excerpts of my interactions with them in this book for the benefit of the readers, to give them a brief window into the lives of some overachieving marathoners. My purpose was for readers to understand that overachievers do not have to be sprinters. I thank them most heartily for their time and their trust in me to share glimpses from their lives. There have been others too, no less remarkable, whose exemplary lives I have quoted for the same purpose. These are: Subash Bose, Ashish Goyal, Mahantesh G. Kivadasannar, V. Mani, T. Raja, P.D.K. Rao, Kim and Kishore S. Rao. I thank them for permitting me to enrich the book with their stories.

There are a number of my close friends and well-wishers who have helped me through various stages of this book. First and foremost, I am hugely indebted to my best friend and wife, Meena. As with all my previous books, she has been instrumental in plodding through my manuscripts, draft after draft. Her perspectives on education and life have contributed greatly to my thinking, and hence the book as well.

I owe a great deal to Sushma Bhalkikar and Nilofer Suleman, who reviewed the first draft for me and gave me some critical comments. Nor can I overlook the ever-smiling T.S. Unnikrishnan, who helped me with certain key sections of the book, particularly chapter 6.

One person who has enriched this book enormously with his critical comments, suggestions and ideas is my editor, Krishan Chopra. Krishan was also the one who edited my earlier book, *Games Indians Play – Why We Are the Way We Are*, under the Penguin banner. Without Krishan's incisive and severe editing, the book would have been much poorer.

I hardly need mention that while the book has benifited immensely from all these excellent people, the shortcomings are all my own.

And lastly, no present-day writing is complete without that *him* or *her* conundrum. I believe in absolute equality of genders. However, I find it distracting to keep using *him* or *her* or *he* or *she* or *S(he)* etc. each time just to sound politically correct or to advertise to the world that I am not a male chauvinist. My experience (or call it my shortcoming, if you will) is that using a plural, though perhaps more gender-neutral, isn't always a workable option. So I have chosen not to use any systematic style on this count and have used whatever pronoun that first came to my mind. If anyone doubts my stance on gender equality, s(he) may feel free to call my wife for testimony! With that I rest my case.

V. RAGHUNATHAN

1   WILL THIS BOOK HELP YOU?

Imagine that you are the parent of an 11- to 15-year-old. When you moved to a new city, he took the entrance tests for two of the 'best' schools in town. But he made it to neither. However, he managed to get into a school that was considered 'good', though not among the 'best'. He appears to be bright, but not necessarily brilliant. His general grasp of school subjects is good, though his performance in examinations is at best just above average. In a class of sixty, he usually manages a rank in the top 20 per cent, but never in the top 5 per cent.

He does not seem to be stressed when it comes to his school work or homework. He has a peculiar habit. He typically sets aside some time for doing his homework; he usually manages to finish the work in this time, but if he cannot, he simply leaves it unfinished and moves on to other things – games or reading some fiction or non-fiction or whatever, even though in his school the reprimand for not completing homework is severe. He is quite prepared to face the consequences.

Though this has not happened often, once or twice when you were helping him with some homework in algebra late at night, to be produced the next morning, he asked you, for example, to 'prove' that $a^2 - b^2 = (a+b)\,(a-b)$ before he would try solving the problems, when actually he was simply expected to apply the formula to solve *them. At that time of the night, you were in no mood to prove the equation and simply asked him to get on with it. As a consequence he did not complete his homework and went to school the next morning sans his assignment.*

He appears to be interested in games, but in a strange way. For instance, he gets his friends in the locality to play all kinds of innovative physical games created by him, but excels in no organized sport at school. More often than not, he is busy collecting and exchanging science fiction books for music CDs and has all kinds of other assorted interests ranging from downloading music for the neighbours from the Internet onto their iPods, to taking his bicycle apart and putting it back when the mood catches him. He frequently participates in a variety of competitive events in the school but rarely wins a prize. He seems to read non-textbook material, even newspapers (mostly sports pages) more than his textbooks. Even when exams are round the corner, he does not seem to change his routine very much. He is inclined to helping his classmates with notes and homework – even those who are ahead of him in the class.

As a parent of this hypothetical kid, what would your response be to the following questions in terms of *Yes* and *No*? (Try to track your responses by writing a Y or an N against each question):

1. Will you exhort him to get more serious about his studies and examinations in order to improve his ranking in the class?
2. Will you chide your kid for not being in the top ten percentile and put him on tuitions to ensure that his academic performance improves?

3. Will the fact that your child frequently participates in a variety of competitive events but rarely wins a prize bother you?

4. Are you tempted to advise your child to complete the homework for now and promise to attend to the principles of the topic another day?

5. Will you try to get him to excel in more organized sports in the school rather than fritter away his energies playing informal games with his friends in the locality?

6. Did you have that little pang of regret that your child missed out on a good start in life by not getting into the best school in the city?

7. Will you directly or indirectly make your child see that unless he improves his academic performance, he may fail to make it through entrance exams to institutions like IIT, AIIMS, NID, etc. ?

8. Will you goad your child into spending more time on textbooks than fiction and other works?

9. Will you from time to time hold up another child who may typically be performing on top of the class as an example to improve the performance of your own child in the next test or examination?

Many of us are bound to veer towards 'Yes' for a majority of the questions because even when our mind knows it should not be so, somewhere deep down, the heart votes to the contrary. That is because whether we acknowledge it or not, a majority of us do view life as a race and when we answer 'No' to the questions, that seems to negate this understanding.

How many Ys did you score? If you scored more than 6, looks like you are an inveterate sprinter. You will perhaps benefit most by reading this book.

Did you manage between 4 and 6? Well, you are like most people – you are conditioned by the world to sprint, even if you do not necessarily believe that life is all about sprinting. You may find some useful tips in this book on a healthier attitude to life – an attitude that could possibly help you get more out of life, for yourself or for your child for that matter.

If you scored 3 or less, you are already a convert. You might as well gift this book to someone else who needs it more!

Now let us come to the question: Is life a race at all? If so, what kind of a race is it?

2 IF LIFE IS A RACE...

*I was running this city marathon. As soon as the race
began, I found myself the last of the runners. It was most
embarrassing. The fellow just ahead of me wisecracked,
'Hi there! What is it like to be the bottom of the heap?' I
replied: 'You really want to know?' and I dropped out...*

—ANONYMOUS

IF YOU ARE LIKE MOST PEOPLE, YOU PROBABLY EXPECT A
lot from yourself. You push yourself hard to stay ahead,
professionally, socially and perhaps every which way. Maybe,
you were always way up there at the top in school and college.
You were the first one to get a campus placement and that
most coveted job. You logged in maximum hours a week in
the company and wanted to be the first one in the batch to
be promoted. You kept it up again and again. You are still
at it, without let. Year after year, you want the best rating in
the company's performance evaluation system. You want that
coveted posting. You once nearly burst a blood vessel when a
promotion was delayed. You strive to be the first one among
your peers to buy that next big car, every three years. You quit
your last job because they would not agree to your proposition
to re-designate you from Regional Head (West) to General

Manager (West). You do not recall when you spent a whole day with your family. You don't remember when you helped a less fortunate man on the street or when you actually heard out a joke told by a five-year-old. Yes, you push yourself hard, very hard indeed. Well, you are just being an average pup – a pushy upwardly mobile professional.

And if you happen to be a parent, you expect no less, and probably more, from your child. Maybe you would be a prouder and a happier parent if your child were among the top performers in the class and outside it. Your tacit expectation of your child is that he will top at everything and crack that mathematics Olympiad and captain the school's cricket and football team. And over and above this, that he would also win the spelling bee, and maybe also walk on water. So high are your expectations perhaps that your body language makes it clear to your kid that if he fails in these expectations, you would be more than somewhat disappointed, and if he succeeds, you would be more than merely happy – you would be ecstatic indeed, and even love the child a dash more. You drive your kid from school to tuitions to swimming classes to tennis lessons. You organize the kid's summer vacation meticulously. Maybe on occasion you have been tempted to compare your kid favourably or unfavourably to some other kid who in your opinion is doing worse or better in studies and sports.

In short, you are in all likelihood an average educated parent, wanting nothing but the best for – and from – your child. If so, you are probably acting like a coach to a sprinter.

AN ASSUMPTION AND AN ASSERTION

Now to be a sprinter is great. To be a sprinter's coach is great as well. But only if the race being run were indeed a sprint. The fact is that the race of life, assuming life is a race at all, is more like a marathon than a sprint. So if your kid is running a marathon, it does little good to train him to be a sprinter. If life is a marathon, the runner needs the qualities of a marathon runner more than the qualities of a sprinter. For that very reason, he needs a marathon coach and not a sprint coach.

I have made one assumption and one assertion above:

I. Assumption: Life is a race
II. Assertion: Given that life is a race, it's a marathon, not a sprint

Now let's take a closer look at the assumption and the assertion.

ASSUMPTION: LIFE IS A RACE

Well, it needn't be. Ideally, it shouldn't be. As a matter of fact, it isn't. But then to treat life not as a race but a wonderful day out on an adventure trek, though idealistically compelling, is unlikely to cut ice with most parents, particularly in India, where competition among children in practically any sphere of life tends to be intense. Why else would most educated parents make their kids hop tuitions before and after school; or want them to solve the question paper all over again at home in an attempt to forecast the examination marks; or expect them to top their class year after year; or look forward to their acing any competition they enter; or make them run from swimming classes to tennis lessons to the cricket ground; or peg all their hopes on having their offspring make it through one of the three-letter national entrance tests as a good start to life?

Even the famous talk-show host, Oprah Winfrey, also a marathon finisher, maintains, 'Running is the greatest metaphor for life…'.[1] We can be safe in assuming that Oprah was referring to the metaphor of running the marathon and not the sprint. Moreover, we probably do regard the run that is life as a race. That is why we talk of getting ahead in life and/or being laggards, or being *numero uno* in this or that.

I have therefore chosen to proceed on the safe assumption that most people do believe that life is a race, given that so much of human happiness is indeed derived not from how well one is doing oneself, but from how much better one is doing in relation to others![2] Wishing to do better than one's peers and emerging tops, either directly for oneself or vicariously through one's offspring, is innate to human nature. If you are the evolved kind who does not regard life as a race at all, well, there is nothing for you but to check if your bookshop will take the book back for a refund.

---

[1] Jennifer Harris and Elwood Watson (ed), *The Oprah Phenomenon, The University Press of Kentucky, 2007*.

[2] What is often referred to in sociological literature in the context of happiness as the Sociological Theory of Relativity.

ASSERTION: IF LIFE IS A RACE AT ALL, IT IS A MARATHON, NOT A SPRINT

We all want to be winners in the race that life is. But what is the nature of the race of life really?

I read a cartoon quip once about a tranquil man standing by a track, watching a cloud of dust in the distance. In the centre of the cloud is a man, astride a horse, galloping towards him. The tranquil man feels a rush of blood in his veins and is contemplating whether or not he should be doing likewise. As the rider approaches, the man asks whither he is headed. And the rider responds, 'I don't know; ask the horse!'

The point of the story is that if life is a race at all, this may not be the way to run it. But the fact is, most of us are in a great rush, often unclear about where we are headed, not unlike our rider. And yet, that is what we frequently do, even with our children. We rush about and we rush them about, not exactly knowing where we are headed and why.

Clearly, any race must have a clear destination. And given that life is a race, we all want to be winners in the race. For this we need to know where the winning line is. And what the nature of the race of life is. Is it more like a sprint or is it more like the marathon? It is this knowledge that will help us to prepare for the race.

There is near-universal agreement that life, taken as a whole, mimics a marathon a lot more than a sprint. A sprint involves a very short distance and lasts a very short time, while a marathon involves a very long distance and lasts very much longer. There are many other differences. And, of course, there are also smaller segments of life that can be compared to a sprint.

For instance, striving single-mindedly to be perennially ahead on the organizational and social ladder may be akin to running one's life as if it were a perpetual sprint. But to balance one's professional life with one's family and close friends, one's hobbies, one's reading or taking time off to climb a hill on a weekend or to go cycling with one's child or taking him to visit an orphanage to teach him that life does not deal the same cards to all, may be akin to running one's life like a marathon.

Similarly, expecting a kid to top the class in every test or exam or activity may be akin to asking the child to run life as though it were a series of sprints. But helping a child to develop holistically, assisting the child in becoming a productive and useful citizen, and giving that child an opportunity to exploit his potential to the fullest and thus achieve fulfilment, is akin to helping the child run his life as if it were a marathon.

If you or your child is running a marathon, whether or not you miss that promotion or miss out on that deal, or whether or not your child topped a particular test or examination, may not be of crucial significance in life, just as whether or not a runner was ahead of the pack at a certain point in the marathon may not be the deciding factor for winning the marathon.

By the same token, the characteristics required for success in a sprint are very different from those required for a marathon.

What are the characteristics that distinguish a sprinter from a marathon runner?

3   SPRINT VERSUS MARATHON

We are different, in essence, from other men. If you want to win something, run 100 metres. If you want to experience something, run a marathon.

—EMIL ZATOPEK, THREE-TIME OLYMPIC GOLD WINNING
LONG-DISTANCE RUNNER (1952)

I F YOU HAVE OBSERVED A GOOD SPRINTER AND A GOOD marathon runner even casually, you would have noticed that the two are as different as chalk and cheese. One is built muscular and beefy for short bursts of high speed, while the other is skinny and light – built for hours of running at a steady pace. One is built for strength, and the other for stamina; one for speed, and the other for endurance. Of course there are many other differences. But whatever they are, it is intuitively obvious to anybody that the two are so different that one cannot do well what the other does. As important as the obvious physical differences are the differences in mental and emotional make-up in the training and preparation for the two. If you want to win a marathon, your training has to be very different from that of a sprinter.

So, what are the key differences between a sprint and a marathon?

SHORT RUN VS LONG RUN

A sprint involves running very short distances, typically under 400 metres, while the marathon is a really long run – 26 miles and 385 yards, or 42.195 km.

FLAT AND STRAIGHT STRETCH VS A TWISTING AND TURNING TRACK WITH UPS AND DOWNS

A sprint track is flat and often straight. The runner hardly needs a variety of skills to negotiate the track. Conditions on the track are fairly uniform. So are the climatic conditions he needs to negotiate. All he has to do is run straight ahead and reach high speed at the earliest and keep up the pace as long as he can, which is not too long.

A marathoner's track may typically twist and turn. It may go up and down over a long distance. Nor would the quality of the ground over which he runs remain constant. His track has a long beginning, a long middle and a long finishing stretch. As a consequence, the runner has to make a constant adjustment for speed depending on the terrain. His running methods may have to account for the hardness of the turf, the weather conditions and such. He needs to decide when to take a break, when to sip that water, when to catch his breath. His race involves many choices and decisions, while that of the sprinter does not.

STRENGTH VS STAMINA

A sprint may last a few seconds. A marathon may take a few hours. Hence the respiratory, cardiovascular and musculoskeletal make-up of sprinters and marathon runners are entirely different. When you look at a sprinter, you would notice that he is rather muscular and built strongly for power, while a marathon runner is typically skinny or lean and built for stamina and endurance. The former is built for rapid burning of calories whereas the latter for slow burning of calories.

ENERGY VS MENTAL TOUGHNESS

A sprinter needs energy to burn oxygen at a rapid pace. He is all about action. In fact, there is very little time – at most a few seconds – for a sprinter to use his head. He has to think with his legs and not mind. He trains himself to give the maximum possible burst of energy in minimum time.

On the other hand, a marathon runner is all about mental strength. For example, after twenty miles or so, many marathon runners 'hit the wall' – a well-known phenomenon when their bodies 'run out of gas'. And this is when the marathon runner switches from his legs to his mind. That is why he trains so carefully to spread his energies evenly through the long race and to bring his mind into play if and when his legs fail.

This does not mean that sprinters do not have strong minds! What we are trying to say is that mental faculties, such as strong willpower, endurance, the never-say-die attitude, patience, timing, mind over body and such attributes have to play a strong and a more sustained role when one is running a long distance race, than during a sprint, since a sprint is over in seconds. The great Paavo Nurmi, a national hero of Finland, who in his time set forty world records, and won nine gold and three silver medals in the Olympics from 1920 to 1928 in twelve events, evidently agrees when he says, 'Mind is everything: muscle – pieces of rubber. All that I am, I am because of my mind.'[1]

Says Jacqueline Gareau, the 1980 Boston Marathon champ, 'The body does not want you to do this. As you run, it tells you to stop but the mind must be strong. You always go too far for your body. You must handle the pain with strategy...It is not age; it is not diet. It is the will to succeed.'[2] And General S. Patton of the US Army, also a 1912 pentathlon Olympian, completes Gareau's quote, as it were, saying, '...You have to make the mind run the body. Never let the body tell the mind what to do. The body will always give up. It is always tired morning, noon, and night. But the body is never tired if the mind is not tired...You've always got to make the mind take over and keep going.'[3]

---

[1] Mark Will Weber, *The Quotable Runner: Great Moments of Wisdom, Inspiration, Wrongheadedness, and Humor*, Breakaway Books, 1999.

[2] Denise Helm quoting Jacqueline Gareau in 'Woman on the Run – Don't tell me to stop running', *Times Colonist*, 15 May 2009.

[3] While the exact source of the quote is unknown, it is available widely on the Net.

A RUSH OF SPEED VS STRATEGIC PERSISTENCE

The sprinter's *mantra* is simple – speed, more speed and even more speed, from the word go – forever focused on remaining ahead of his competitors. He is typically intolerant of someone overtaking him as there is practically no time left for him to catch up. Each competitor overtaking him is an immediate threat to his winning the race.

For a long-distance runner, however, it is all about strategy and persistence. How to get into a rhythmic pace that can be kept up not for the next few seconds but for the next few hours? How best to conserve energy? How much water to drink? When to change one's pace? At what point to draw on that hidden reserve of energy? How to get the mind to bear on the run, when the legs are beginning to give way? Whether to run at an even pace or start slow in the first hour and accelerate in the last? How to manage that cramp in the stomach with minimal loss of time? How to manage the pain?

What is more, for most of the race, someone overtaking him does not bother him. He runs his race with patience, confident in his game-plan and the steadiness of his pace, knowing and trusting his stamina, abilities and timing, sure that he will catch up sooner or later with those who went on ahead.

Clearly a sprinter will not ever be able to complete a marathon. He will burn out in the first few hundred metres.

By the same token, a marathon runner is hardly built to run the sprint. His physiology and psychology are all about slow burning of oxygen in a steady and sustained manner.

VISIBLE PROGRESS VS NOT-SO-VISIBLE PROGRESS

The sprinter's progress through the race is visible to the most casual observer. Within seconds of the start, it is easy to tell the likely winner.

In case of a marathon runner, however, it is not clear who the winner will be. Being ahead of another runner for most of the race hardly implies that the one ahead will necessarily also finish ahead. It is difficult to tell from the relative positions of the runners in the first 10 to 15 km as to who is likely to win the race. In fact, there may be little correlation between being ahead very early in the race and being the final winner.

END VS THE PATH

A sprinter is unwaveringly focused on the finishing point every second of his dash. His finishing post is clearly in sight every moment and straight ahead all the time. He knows exactly where he is headed and there is very little doubt that he will get there in a trice. For this reason, there is no particular fun in the process of running per se, as there is nothing to enjoy en route, except perhaps a rush of wind on the face.

In contrast, a marathon runner, for most of the race, needs to focus only on his trail and not the finishing post. The trail, if beautiful, by itself could be a source of enjoyment as well. He can take that breather en route, or slow down for a drink of water.

As for the finishing line, it is never in sight for the marathoner, until he is almost there, though he knows broadly where he is headed. He will need all his mental strength and control to get there. If he gets too dehydrated or burns his energy too fast, or his mental toughness fails him, he may not get there. The reality is that there is an element of uncertainty as to whether he will finish at all. It's the trail that stays in his mind most of the time, much more than the finishing post.

WINNING VS RUNNING THE COURSE

For a marathoner, having endured the distance and bettered his own time is a great source of satisfaction in itself. For him, the very experience of running and finishing the marathon successfully can be its own reward, unlike for a sprinter, for whom finishing first is all that matters. For the sprinter, there is little consolation in merely completing the race. If he does not win the race, there is little joy in the running.

Sister Marion Irvine, who at the age of 54 qualified for the 1984 US Olympic Marathon trials at 2 hrs and 51 seconds, calls the marathon a more or less spiritual experience. She says, 'It's elevating and humbling at the same time. Running along a beach at sunrise with no other footprints in the sand, you realize the vastness of creation, your own insignificant space in the plan, how tiny you really are...'[4]

---

[4] Quoted in *In Stride*, The Arlington Striders Running Club Newsletter, May/June, 2009.

COMPETING WITH OTHERS VS COMPETING WITH SELF

A sprinter is constantly focused on others, lest they outrun him. If he finds someone gaining on him, he strains that much extra to remain ahead. It is competition with others that guides his run. He strives to remain ahead of the competitors practically throughout the race. He is externally driven.

In contrast, a marathon, because of the distance, is as much a race against oneself as against competitors. In focusing on himself, the runner runs against his own past timing. He wills himself to continue when his entire body rebels against continuing. The relative position of his competitors vis-à-vis himself is largely irrelevant to him. He is merely trying to maintain and follow his own rhythm and running plan. Essentially, he is inward-looking. He begins to think of overtaking competitors only towards the end of the race.

START VS FINISH

For a sprinter, a good start is most crucial. The block has to be tightly in place. His take-off posture has to be just right. His take-off timing has to be perfect. The micro-second advantage from being off the block just as the pistol shot goes off may make all the difference. In other words, a bad start almost invariably spells the sprinter's disaster in the race. If he is not quick enough upon take-off, chances are he loses the race right with the first step. For him, well begun is half-done.

On the other hand, for a marathon runner, a good start is practically irrelevant. In fact, except for keeping a steady pace, he hardly needs to worry about anything else, till he is somewhere close to the finish. It is only when nearing the finishing line that a marathon runner tries to better his own average pace. For him, all's well that end's well – the end being completing the marathon.

Says a world record holder of the marathon, Robert de Castella of Australia, 'The marathon is about being in contention over the last 10 km. That's when it's about what you have in your core. You have run all the strength, all the superficial fitness out of yourself, and it really comes down to what's left inside you. To be able to draw deep and pull something out of yourself is one of the most tremendous things about the marathon.'[5]

COMPETITION VS CAMARADERIE

Marathons are frequently run for causes and attract amateurs in large numbers in an atmosphere of fun and revelry. It is not unusual to see tens of thousands of people running a marathon for a cause. This is hardly typical of sprints.

The atmosphere of a marathon is often one of camaraderie and amity, unlike a sprint which has an aura of serious rivalry. One can almost imagine a marathon runner helping a co-runner complete the course, while that is hardly imaginable in a sprint.

---

[5] Quoted in TheFinalSprint.com (whose Founder and Editor, Adam Jacobs, an enthusiastic supporter of distance running in the US, unexpectedly died at the young age of 24 on 22 May 2009).

In short, running a marathon calls for optimizing across several characteristics, while a sprint essentially calls for maximizing speed.

The characteristics required in a sprinter vis-à-vis a marathon runner should, it is to be hoped, convince us that if life is a race at all, it mimics a marathon a lot more than it mimics a sprint.

> *How do we prepare ourselves or our child to run the marathon of life?*

4   CHILD – THE PARENT OF MAN

A martial arts student went to his teacher and said earnestly, 'I am devoted to studying your martial arts system. How long will it take me to master it?' The teacher's reply was casual. 'Ten years.' Impatiently, the student asked, 'But I want to master it faster than that. I will work very hard. I will practise every day; ten hours or more a day, if I have to. How long will it take then?' The teacher thought for a moment and said, 'Twenty years!'

—ANONYMOUS

CAN THE CHARACTERISTICS OF SPRINTERS VERSUS marathon runners help us understand ourselves better? Since we started with the example of a hypothetical child in chapter 1, let us continue with it, remembering all the time that the essential arguments hold as much for us adults as for the hypothetical child.

UNDERSTANDING THE HYPOTHETICAL CHILD

Let us say we are trying to understand the nature of the

hypothetical child we described in chapter 1. The table below lists the broad characteristics of the child.

Nature	Characteristic
a. He appears to be somewhat laid-back, but is a steady and a consistent performer – does not exert himself beyond a point; he chooses what he will spend his time on.	He seems to place steadiness, endurance and patience over speed, and makes conscious choices – a marathon runner.
b. He has some fine and deep qualities – for example, he is innovative, helpful, well read, has wide interests.	He has more not-so-visible attributes than visible ones like topping the class or captaining the school team – a marathon runner.
c. He has strong moral fibre, but not the steam required for immediate action – is willing to accept the consequences (reprimand) for his actions (not doing the homework); helps his friends and is not perturbed if they perform better than himself.	He shows strength of character – a marathon runner.
d. He is comprehension-driven rather than end-result driven and steady – is more interested in understanding the principle of a subject than in completing the homework.	He seems to be focused on the trail (process) rather than the finishing line (end) – a marathon runner.

e. He is not particularly bothered about where he stands vis-à-vis his peers – seems to be comfortable being amongst the top 15 of the 60.	He is more focused on self than on competition – a marathon runner.
f. He isn't brilliant, but he seems to be bright enough – missed out getting into the best school, but made it to the next rung.	A good start foregone – not a big handicap if he is a marathon runner.

We find that our hypothetical child is intrinsically perhaps more of a marathon runner than a sprinter. Good for the child, since that is what he is running.

WHAT KIND OF PARENTS ARE WE?

Well, let us take a look at how we responded to the nine questions in chapter 1 pertaining to our hypothetical kid.

A. IF OUR ANSWERS TO QUESTIONS 1, 2 OR 3 WERE YES

The questions were:

- Will you exhort him to get more serious about his studies and examinations in order to improve his ranking in the class?;
- Will you chide your kid for not being in the top ten percentile and put him on tuitions to ensure that his academic performance improves?;

- Will the fact that your child frequently participates in a variety of competitive events but rarely wins a prize bother you?

We probably expect and urge our kid to top every test, exam and every sport. We possibly berate the kid for his lower level of performance – either directly by rebuke or indirectly through high expectations. We probably make it clear to the child that he must show immediate strength and speed, while he seems to be a kid given to steady, enduring and patient habits. It is not as if he does not work hard. He simply works at a variety of things – things besides school. He plays, he reads, he participates in a variety of events, he has hobbies, he is quite good at computers, he reads a variety of material. He is not a laggard by a far stretch. But from our perspective, he is too slow. That's because we want him to run a sprint, while he is running a marathon.

B. IF OUR ANSWER TO QUESTION 4 WAS YES

The question was:

- Are you tempted to advise your child to complete the homework for now and promise to attend to the principles of the topic another day?

We are probably impressing upon our child that quick-fix solutions and being perennially in a rush are greater virtues than method and patience. We would rather that the kid took a short cut and escaped punishment than be true to self and accepted the consequences. Our emphasis seems to be short-term-result oriented rather than rather than laying the foundations for seeking knowledge in the long haul. We are probably expecting the child to run each year as if it were a sprint. In the process, we are expecting our child to run the entire 42 km at a breakneck pace, as if a marathon can be won by splitting it into a series of sprints.

C. IF OUR ANSWER TO QUESTION 5 WAS YES

The question was:

• Will you try to get him to excel in more organized sports in the school rather than fritter away his energies playing informal games with his friends in the locality?

We are probably placing a premium on energy and force over character building. We may be ignoring the fact that our child is perhaps showing spontaneous leadership and team-building qualities in rounding up his friends and leading them to play games devised by him. We may be overlooking the fact that it is through forming and leading his own team that a child cultivates the spirit of leadership, team spirit, friendship, initiative and fun, besides learning to fight and forget, and accepting others for what they are. Besides, we may be killing the spirit of innovation and leadership in the child who develops fanciful games and has the ability to get others to play them – a trait that in years to come may translate into pursuing an innovative and entrepreneurial idea and building an organization that will call for a team to be assembled and motivated to work. Unless our child is destined to grow into a major sports personality (which he is not, given that he does not particularly excel in any sport), his informal games among his group of friends may be far more beneficial to his character building in the long haul than any specific achievement in formal sports.

D. IF OUR ANSWER TO QUESTION 6 OR 7 WAS YES

The questions were:

- Did you have that little pang of regret that your child missed out on a good start in life by not getting into the best school in the city?;
- Will you directly or indirectly make your child see that unless he improves his academic performance, he may fail to make it through entrance exams to institutions like IIT, AIIMS, NID, etc. ?

We are perhaps placing too much emphasis on a good start. We do not seem to realize that a good start is just that. It is crucial in a sprint but not in a marathon. There is little correlation between getting the best start in a marathon and winning it, or for that matter between getting a bad start and not winning it, as long as we do not trip and break a bone right at the start. Maybe a good start does put us ahead of the pack to begin with, and even wins the race if it is a sprint. But in a marathon, soon a host of other factors, like rhythm, endurance, mental toughness, metabolic rate, the climatic conditions, take over and the good start is of little relevance.

It's the same with topping school examinations – this has no established correlation with meaningful success in later life. In fact, most successful people (we are not referring to child prodigies here) are more likely to have been well-rounded students than students who necessarily always topped their academic curriculum – something that occupies the mind of most parents. Our child may appear to have missed out on the top school, but it's like having missed out on a good start in a marathon – it really does not matter much. In life, it's really not all that important, as long as he is getting a decent education. From here on, a host of other factors will determine whether he wins the race of life or not. It's the same with the IIT entrance examination – by gaining or not gaining entry into an IIT, we are merely getting or not getting a good start in a marathon, no more, no less. Even if one didn't make it to such an institution, there is plenty of time and track left to catch up.

E. IF OUR ANSWER TO QUESTION 8 WAS YES

The question was:

- Will you goad your child into spending more time on textbooks than fiction and other works?

Our preoccupation with textbooks is probably a pointer to our pre-occupation with the finishing line – namely exams – rather than a focus on the trail – the process of learning. What good education should aim to do is to create in a child sufficient interest and curiosity to pick up a book to learn; to look at the world around and wonder; to observe and get curious; to question; to experiment; to analyse; to discover; to construct and create knowledge; and to use knowledge constructively. What that knowledge is or what that curiosity is about is largely irrelevant. Seeking any knowledge; being curious about anything; making or constructing whatever –

that's the key. Once a child makes a habit of these, the most important function of education is already achieved.

To come back to the scenario, let's face it. For a youngster, a textbook is not the most exciting reading material. There is learning beyond textbooks, perhaps much more than we usually think. As long as the child is not ignoring his curriculum entirely, he should be encouraged to read as widely as possible and not discouraged. Our hypothetical kid is certainly doing reasonably well even in the school – after all he is not a laggard. He is among the top 20 percentile of the class without killing himself at the altar of the school curriculum. He reads whatever interests him. He is in the habit of reading the newspaper, even if it's only the sports news. In due course, when his interests shift to other areas, he is sure to satiate those interests from a more wholesome reading of the newspapers; who knows, in time, he may want to contribute his views to them as well – something not possible if he weren't intimate with the concept of a newspaper to begin with. He is concentrating on running the race, like a good marathon runner. His finishing line is far away and yet we are forcing him to be focused on a finishing line called the next test or exam.

F. IF OUR ANSWER TO QUESTION 9 WAS YES

The question was:

- Will you from time to time hold up another child who may typically be performing on top of the class as an example to improve the performance of your own child in the next test or examination?

We are perhaps too focused on competition vis-à-vis others, rather than letting our child concentrate on himself. The nature of competition in a marathon is quite different from that in a sprint, even though in both the races, the objective is to emerge the winner. In a sprint, we are obliged throughout the short race, not merely to run fast ourselves, but also keep an eye behind us to ensure no one else is overtaking us. Such is obviously not the case in a marathon, where except towards the end of the race, we are always trying to run against ourselves, and being overtaken does not matter for most of the race. Comparing our child to another is therefore putting our priorities wrong.

And that is not all either. In creating such a competitive spirit, we are also negating the value of cooperation and teamwork – attributes that are key to life.

It is evident that the more the 'Yeses' to those questions, the more likely that as parents we are intrinsically sprint coaches. If so, it is like expecting the child to break up a marathon into a series of 100-metre segments, which he should run at the pace of a sprinter. If we are such parents, we must realize that this is simply too unreasonable and untenable an expectation. The best of them can crack under the expectation.

Our normal professional lifespan lasts some 40-odd years between childhood and effective end of peak career at around 50 plus. To emerge a winner at the end of these 40-odd professional years, the parent needs to ready the child to treat the race of life in its proper perspective. The parent's answers to most of those questions need to be in the negative! Of course that is not to say that you ought not to gently prod a laid-back child to work harder, or a child with a very short attention span to concentrate more seriously, or to learn at times to balance the short term with the long term. Our concern here is with the parents whose compulsive 'Yeses' to those questions exert serious pressures on their children.

To remind ourselves once again, the example of the child was merely incidental. We also need to ask ourselves how we are running our own races in life!

DR KALLAM ANJI REDDY

It may be of some interest for us to take a look at the mini bio-sketch of Dr Kallam Anji Reddy – the man who has put India's pharmaceutical industry on the world frontier, and the man who set up Dr Reddy's Labs or Dr Reddy's Laboratories Ltd.

The son of a fairly well-to-do turmeric farmer from a village called Tadepalli in Andhra Pradesh, Kallam Anji Reddy went to a local school called the Annapotanna Bold High School, before moving on to a junior college by name Hindu College in Guntur. He scored 355/600 (59.16 per cent) in the State Board and then went on to Andhra Christian College in the same town for a B.Sc. in chemistry, and unsure of his performance in the finals, dropped out to appear again in a supplementary.

Apparently, the only anxiety Dr Reddy's parents ever showed towards his education was to move Anji to his grandmother's home for his primary schooling, about 8 km away from his home in Tadepalli, as his father did not want the eight-year-old Anji crossing the Krishna river every day to attend school. Thereafter little Anji was on his own.

A fairly mischievous diminutive little fellow with a whole

bunch of friends, often cutting school prayer to indulge in
some prank with his gang of friends, Anji was your average
village boy. If anything at all was remarkable about him,
it was his sharp memory and the fact that he was given to
reading – reading not so much his textbooks, but reading in
general. He was seriously given to detective novels and the
odd Rabindranath Tagore and Sarat Chandra in his mother
tongue, Telugu. But more than anything else, Dr Reddy
believes he was a friends' man even as a youngster. He had
a wide circle of friends whom he was genuinely fond of. He
spent much time in their company. Being small in size did
not prevent him from holding his own. Recalls Dr Reddy,
someone returning from the US had gifted the school with
a set of baseball equipment. And so the school's main sport
was baseball! Little Anji developed his own ingenious style
of play. While other players used maximum force to hit out
at the ball and run to first base, Anji would let the ball come
on to the bat and drop down near his own feet, and by the
time the pitcher or the catcher came running to retrieve the
ball, he would manage to reach the first base! Other than this,
Anji, cocooned in his little village, showed little promise of
his future accomplishments.

He did reasonably well through school, more often than not
depending on the notes of his friends, but capitalizing on his
excellent memory. For his school finals, he moved to a junior
college in Guntur and secured a high second class – though
still managing to top the school. Of course, those were the days
prior to the '95 per cent-plus' era. Even a first class was much
cherished. And yet, even accounting for that, his performance
was nothing spectacular.

Young Anji moved to a degree college in the same town and even though his first love seems to have been languages, somehow he found himself opting for chemistry. Dr Reddy thinks this is easily explained. The college had a wonderful teacher in chemistry who managed to teach a subject usually not taught too well in schools, in a manner that ignited his early interest in the subject. Anji was still banking on his friends' notes and his memory to help him along. Thanks to the superior educational standards of the time and to his excellent lecturer, Anji got to read the best of classics in chemistry (as probably did every student those days). In the final year, he suddenly developed cold feet after he thought he had botched the examination in one subject. He thought it perfectly fine to wait another six months and appear in the supplementary exams. Dr Reddy recalls with a chuckle that later he found that he had cleared that subject with 62 per cent marks! Nothing very remarkable about our caterpillar so far. His visible metamorphosis to a butterfly would happen many years later.

Anji is not a sprinter by a far shot. When he finally graduated with a degree in chemistry, he moved on to join Bombay University for a B.Sc (Tech) in pharmaceutical and fine chemicals. From there, he went to National Chemical Laboratory, Pune for his Masters, but ended up picking up his PhD.

His early love for languages seems to have come in handy here. In those days, learning the German language was compulsory for all students pursuing a career in science. Dr Reddy recalls that even though he does not remember working too hard for this German examination, he seems to have combined his language skills and some 'smart working' – as opposed to only hard-working – to get through the examination in the very first attempt, even though some of his more diligent colleagues do not seem to have done so!

Of course, here we must factor in the fact that Dr Reddy could not have reached where he has in life without being an extremely intelligent individual. In him, the brilliance may be wrapped in modesty to the extent that Dr Reddy believes even today that it all happened rather easily!

With a PhD under his belt, Anji, in the spirit and influence of socialism of the times, joined the state-owned Indian Drugs and Pharmaceuticals Ltd in 1969. He spent the next six years at IDPL learning as much as he could about bulk drug manufacturing. This was the era of the public sector giant, and the State Trading Corporation loomed large over anything that needed importing. Among their imports were all bulk drugs. As Anji learnt the ropes, what prima facie appeared to be a China Wall, namely all bulk drugs being state-controlled (making it extremely difficult for the private sector to make an entry), also appeared to be a great opportunity.

Opportunities are shy maidens. They are seldom visible to the less alert. It's a keen eye that detects an opportunity. Perhaps, this is where Anji's freewheeling childhood came in handy, to enable him to see life without constraints and blinkers. With a more restrained education, focused on a 'career', he may well have missed seeing the opportunity.

Anji figured that he had learnt as much about bulk drugs as there was to be learnt at IDPL.

He had around that time worked out that he could himself make a certain drug that was at that time being imported. What is more, being an import-substitution product, he would not even have to expend too much energy or capital marketing the drug. STC would merely hand out supply licences (it was still the licence-permit raj, remember) to Anji.

And thus in 1976 Dr Reddy founded his first company, Uniloids Ltd (the 'loids' being the suffix coming from 'alkaloids') – a rather modernistic name for a company of that time!

In 1980 Dr Reddy set up the Standard Organics Ltd, and the flagship Dr Reddy's Labs in 1984. The Indian pharmaceutical industry had been redefined. Dr Reddy's Labs went on to turn the Indian bulk drugs industry from dependence on imports to self-reliance in a matter of a decade or so. The company went to drug discovery research just as the country was unshackling itself from the licence-permit raj in the 1990s. The turn of the century saw the company – the first Asian company ever outside Japan – list on the New York Stock Exchange. Today (in 2009) Dr Reddy's Labs is vying for the top slot among India's largest pharmaceutical companies.

Dr Reddy serves as a member of the Prime Minister's Council on Trade and Industry. He is also among the most decorated scientific entrepreneurs in the country. But what is of interest to us here is that by any reckoning, Dr Reddy comes out as a long-distance runner. He has been a man who didn't ever sprint. He was a steady, but not necessarily a spectacular, student. He took reasonably well to science in college and pursued the line. Rather than get distracted with alternatives like an IIT or an IIM, he stuck to his core area of interest, namely chemistry and drugs. He steadily added to his learning at a PSU, and at an appropriate time, read the environment and capitalized on the opportunity steadily. He didn't necessarily have a vision or a dream of what he wanted to be as a kid. And yet, he was focused enough to know just when the time was right for him to surge ahead. His parents, whether by design or by accident, left him alone to flower in his own way. And Anji Reddy did precisely that. Yes, Kallam Anji Reddy is our quintessential long-haul runner.

He had the inner character to stay with his area of strength. He didn't necessarily know exactly where he was going to end up, and yet, he enjoyed his journey all the way. He capitalized admirably upon his two major strengths – his friendly nature and his excellent memory. He used his memory well to master the science of chemistry and drug making. His other most important early attribute, namely his friendly disposition, is what he probably used as his second-most important capital in his journey of entrepreneurship.

Reflecting on Dr Anji Reddy's background, nothing comes out more strongly than the fact that more often than not, it is not possible to judge the potential of a child very early. Dr Reddy didn't exhibit any early indication of his greatness to come. His parents did not particularly worry one way or the other, other than let their son have as decent an education as they could afford. The child Anji grew up as a reasonably balanced and steady kid. But even when he was entering college he had no great clarity on what he wanted to do or where he wanted to go. The visions and the dreams came much later. In Dr Reddy's own opinion, he probably reflected upon and formed his entrepreneurial dream while at IDPL, watching the Indian bulk drugs environment. Had he been racing very hard all the time trying to scale the corporate ladder, he would have probably failed to see the opportunity. Or he might have been so focused on the next promotion that he may not have seen the entrepreneurial opportunity at all.

In fact, Dr Reddy didn't have a grand start in life. He didn't start life from a city. He wasn't a conventionally brilliant student. He didn't study at a fancy school, college or university. His first job wasn't with an MNC. He almost never had a target to get a certain percentage of marks, or crack a certain test, or join up a particular college. He didn't think he needed an MBA, though deep down he was an entrepreneur. Even after joining professional life, he wasn't in a rat race. He didn't job hop. Instead, he concentrated on learning the ropes. He read. Even if the reading was predominantly fiction, he enjoyed the very act of reading. This would stand him in good stead in later life. He had a good memory and he made use of that asset. He jogged along at a steady pace, took time to reflect, ascertained his strengths and studied the opportunities the environment of the time offered. And finally he found his interest, which he developed into a passion. It is not difficult to imagine that no matter where little Anji had studied, no matter what discipline he had pursued, he would have found his natural level.

One feels inclined to say that an average parent, with a child like Anji, is unlikely to have foreseen that he had an epic runner growing up in the family! Amidst a crowd of sprinters even in those days, Dr Reddy was unquestionably a marathon runner. Wittingly or unwittingly, his parents left him alone to forge his own path, at his own pace. He could so easily have been forced into a sprint and steered away from chemistry by a present-day parent!

> *Well then, don't you need to know yourself better so that you can get yourself, or if you are a parent, your child, in better readiness to take on life?*

5 DEVELOPING THE RIGHT ATTITUDE TO LIFE

If you are running a marathon: 'Set your own pace. If you black out after five minutes, you are probably running too fast. If a workman from the city comes by and paints you green, you may be running too slow.'

—A JOGGING TIP[1]

LET US CONSIDER A POSER. SUPPOSING YOU COULD transform yourself into a student with the wave of a wand or mail-order a kid for yourself, which of the following two would you prefer?

i. A kid with a good grasp on a subject and able to internalize it for application in life, but not able to reproduce the learning verbatim in an examination as usually expected by examiners? This may compromise your grades, or

---

[1] 'Eight Jogging Tips', *Prairie Inn Harriers Newsletter*, December 1980.

ii. One who can pick up a subject superficially and have
     an excellent short-term memory which will be good
     enough to memorize a subject long enough to reproduce
     the answers in the examination and score the highest
     grades?

Even though most of us may say we want the first option,
don't we, as parents, often end up promoting the latter option
in our kids? Aren't we often disproportionately hung up on
examination performance? Why else would most educated
parents enlist their children in various coaching classes for
select institutions starting at 5 a.m.? Why do we regiment not
only our own lives, but also those of our children, their daily
routines, their sports, their internships, their summer vacations
with the thoroughness of dictators?

Often our own lives are no less of a mad rush – a rush for
that next promotion, a rush for that big bonus, that fancy
assignment, that job, and so on. But what is worse is that not
only do we do to our children what we do to ourselves, we also
expect from them, what we failed to achieve ourselves!

SHAPING A CHILD'S PERSONA

Most educated Indian parents have turned into sprint
coaches for their children. Perhaps this is owing to the high
'competitive pressures' arising out of sheer population pressure
in schools, colleges and jobs. It is therefore important for us
to understand certain basic differences between a short-term
and long-term orientation in life. Such an understanding will
help us shape our own as well as our children's attitude to life
better.

WELL BEGUN MAY BE HALF DONE — BUT THAT IS MORE SO IN A DASH

As long as a long-distance runner does not start with a fracture or a sprained ankle or such other disastrous beginning, an average start is good enough. It is the same for us or our child. As long as a child is going to a reasonably good school, is well adjusted, takes a healthy interest in everything, enjoys his school, is fond of his teachers, and has wide and spontaneous interests and is brought up in an environment of high social confidence and trust, that is a good enough start for winning the race of life.

Pushing children unnaturally to strive for the 'best' school in town, or the most-difficult-to-get-into college or institution, or to be at the top of the university, college, school or the class right through their educational career may be good for parents' egos, but not necessarily for children's overall development. These good starts are at best that – good starts, which may have large significance in a sprint, but hardly in a cross-country run.

But the problem is, even if the mind accepts that a great start is not crucial to winning a marathon, the heart is unwilling. Unnatural will be the parent who does not feel a sense of insecurity if their child does not show some early promise. In fact, we all harbour a degree of insecurity in ourselves and the promise of seeing early success in one's child helps allay the feeling.

So what is the best start parents can give to their children? Ideally, parents should try and spot a child's natural inclinations and reasonably encourage those inclinations to a point where the child becomes aware of them. Such encouragement has its natural rewards for the child as well as the parents. We may note that it is hardly difficult to spot the inclinations of an exceptionally gifted child. A young Ravi Shankar or Sachin Tendulkar or a young Viswanathan Anand will leave you in no doubt about their early talents and it takes a lot to keep them from blossoming! So in our discussion to follow, we should be clear that we are not referring to such outliers, who are easily identified. Our subject of discussions here is the average child.

When a child, though not an outlier, has identifiable potential in some direction, a parent may well nudge him to work more concertedly in that direction, apart from the ordinary routine of schooling and learning. But they will do well to let the child become a self-starter in that direction rather than push the child hard against his wishes in a misplaced assessment of that potential. Such undue pressure can often backfire. The child can as easily back off from where you are trying to push him. The nudging should essentially be in the form of encouragement and support for enhancing the child's performance in the general direction of his interests. This is likely to introduce the child to the joys of constructive competition.

But often, parents also have to deal with children who may not show the potential to excel in any particular field early in life and perhaps a large percentage of children fall in this category. What should parents do in such cases? Perhaps the best thing to do would be to let the child develop into a well-rounded individual. All these measures are likely to prove far more effective head starts than having them go to the best school in town and controlling their lives tightly for better performance in exams. This is not to say that a desire to excel is not a desirable trait to impart. It is. But the excellence should come more from the desire to excel one's own performance rather than competing against others. This is perhaps what success and excellence in life is all about. And what could be more important than to prepare one's child for success and excellence in life?

A SUCCESSFUL LIFE

This, of course, begs the question: What does success in life mean? Is success all about making as much money as possible? Is success about being as famous as possible? Is success about being as powerful as possible? It is true that success often brings in its wake money and/or fame and/or power – often one of these three being capable of being converted into the other. According to the American novelist Thomas Wolfe, 'You have reached the pinnacle of success as soon as you become uninterested in money, compliments, or publicity!' Well, you may become 'successful' earlier if you cease to chase money, compliments and publicity earlier! But the fact is, these come more as consequences of doing something well (success) and are not goals of success. And when you overlay happiness over success, the definition of success gets trickier, because it can be argued that happiness is the key to success, success is not the key to happiness!

Consider this. Would you really believe that every rich, famous and powerful person is 'successful' in life? What about those corrupt policemen or the civil servants or the IT czars who are in the national news and police custody for having amassed crores in wealth through corruption, illegal means, or fraud? Would you call them 'successful', even assuming the law never caught up with them? We have a number of worthies masquerading as leaders in our parliament and legislative assemblies, with murder, rape and kidnapping charges pending against them. Would you call them successful, in the sense that you would want your child to take them as role models? As for 'famous', well, Paris Hilton is famous. How many of us would want our daughters to adopt her as a role model? Can she be really called *successful*, even if she is well known (for all the wrong reasons)? More importantly, can a Paris Hilton's lifestyle be a route to anyone's happiness in the serious sense of the word? Is happiness the key to success or success the key to happiness?

As a corollary, would you also really believe that anybody who is neither terribly rich, nor famous, nor powerful, is a failure in life? To make a point, let us consider this physicist, Dr P.D.K. Rao, who returned from the US some thirty years ago, giving up a very lucrative career, and settled in a small village in Andhra Pradesh. He set up a small non-government organization, the Sodhana Charitable Trust, (NGO) which essentially ensures that every village kid in the surrounding villages goes to school. He has committed his life to this cause and has perhaps made a difference to the lives of hundreds of children over the years. He has been adorned by no government award, though he is known and respected by all educationists, and many civil servants. He is not rich. His name may ring no bell in many minds. But he is a happy and satisfied man, committed to serving the poorest of the poor in a remote area. Would you call him a failure in life?

Perhaps then, the best way to understand success in life is to understand it as a life led following one's passion to the point where one's achievements and contribution to society, in whatever field, earn one the respect of good, honourable and knowledgeable people. More often than not, a life thus led also brings in its wake most of the reasonable comforts in life.

To understand what we mean by passion, let us recall Sister Marion Irvine, who, at 54, qualified for the 1984 US Olympic marathon trials at 2 hrs and 51 seconds. She remains the oldest woman ever to have clocked such a time in a marathon. Sister Marion was a nun who resided at Dominican Convent College in San Rafael, California. What motivated her to accomplish the feat? She wanted to give up smoking, lose weight and become healthier. And hence she wanted to take up long-distance running. However, given her sundry duties, it was not easy for her to find the necessary time. She would borrow shorts and shoes from a gymnasium's lost-and-found section and go for brief walks and jogs surreptitiously. As she achieved her goals and her true talents surfaced, she turned public with her jogging. Today, she is a human rights activist, a promoter of social justice for the Dominican Sisters and a highly regarded motivational speaker, and is listed in Wikipedia. Now here is an example of passion turned into success.

Bessie Stanley, the nineteenth-century poetess, the author of the poem 'Success', puts the meaning of 'success' in the best possible words[2]:

---

[2]   The quote is often attributed, perhaps wrongly, to Ralph Waldo Emerson.

He has achieved success who has lived well, laughed often and loved much; who has gained the respect of intelligent men and the love of little children; who has filled his niche and accomplished his task; who has left the world better than he found it, whether by an improved poppy, a perfect poem, or a rescued soul; who has never lacked appreciation of earth's beauty or failed to express it; who has always looked for the best in others and given them the best he had; whose life was an inspiration; whose memory a benediction.

She does not refer to money, fame or power as goals or ingredients of success. The legendary ballerina, Anna Pavlova, echoes the same sentiments when she says, 'To follow without halt, one aim; there is the secret of success. And success? What is it? I do not find it in the applause of the theatre; it lies rather in the satisfaction of accomplishment.'

HOW GOOD A START TO LIFE DO THE TOP SCHOOLS PROVIDE?

Many of our national institutions are excellent institutions. Most students who get into these institutions are extremely bright. But this hardly implies that every student who is bright will necessarily get into these institutions. Or that a student who does not get into one of them is not bright. There could be many reasons for making or not making it into these institutions. Firstly, what with institutions of excellence not being all that many in number, the demand for admission into them far outstrips the seats available, so that the number of extremely bright students competing for seats may be several times the number of seats available. And no matter how bright, when competing against other, equally bright, people, there is always a random factor that could play against you on a given day. What is more, the nature of many of the competitive tests is such that they may not necessarily be the best barometers of intelligence. The typical tests are of the rapid-fire kind, putting the students under severe time constraint – not necessarily the best way to measure intelligence. Further, increasingly, coaching classes take away the discriminating ability of the entrance tests to sift the bright from the not-so-bright. As a consequence, it is possible for a not-so-bright individual well versed in the art of taking objective-type examinations to clear an entrance exam which a very bright and well-rounded youngster, unconditioned by coaching classes, may not. And yet, it could be said with conviction that the well-rounded youngster holds greater promise in the long run.

This means that if a youngster can make it to one of these Ivy League (I use the term broadly, though it refers to a set of colleges in the US) institutions in the normal course, good for him. But conditioning a youngster to gain admission to such institutions by prolonged training in tutorial classes at the expense of an all-round development may be a retrograde move. The cost of such a head start may exceed the benefits.

Not every CEO comes with a degree from an Ivy League institution. Far from it. According to Carol Hymowitz – who has been an editorial director of *Forbes* and a senior editor of the *Wall Street Journal* – in one of her columns, 'The college diplomas of the nation's top executives tell an intriguing story: Getting to the corner office has more to do with leadership talent and a drive for success than it does with having an undergraduate degree from a prestigious university.'[3]

Apparently a large majority of the CEOs in the US went to the state universities and not to the Ivy League private ones. For example, the world's second richest man, Warren Buffet, CEO of Berkshire Hathaway, graduated from the University of Nebraska-Lincoln; A.G. Lafley, CEO of Proctor & Gamble, graduated from Hamilton College in New York; Lee Scot, CEO of Walmart, went to the Pittsburg State University, Kansas; Paul Otellini, CEO of Intel, went to the University of San Francisco; Rex Tillerson, CEO of Exxon Mobil, attended the University of Texas-Austin. The list is long.

Most interestingly, Hymowitz also says in the same article, 'This information should help allay the anxieties of many parents and their college-bound children who believe admission to a top-ranked school with a powerful alumni network is a prerequisite to success in the upper echelons of business management.'[4]

Incidentally, closer home, Narayana Murthy of Infosys got his undergraduate degree from a lesser known National Institute of Engineering, University of Mysore; G. Mallikarjuna Rao of the GMR Group went to a village school and was an engineering graduate from Andhra University, Vizag;

---

[3] Carol Hymowitz, 'Path to the Corner Office Starts at a State School,' As provided by CareerJournal.com in http://encarta. msn.com

[4] Source: http://online.wsj.com/public/article/ SB1158 53818747665842-ZqcThW_76BozMT1wgzstA1afvh8_2008 0510.html (Last accessed on 8 January 2010.)

Shiv Nadar of HCL fame graduated from PSG College of Technology, Coimbatore; S. Ramadorai of TCS started with a B.Sc in Physics from Delhi University; Dr Anji Reddy of Dr Reddy's Laboratories, as we mentioned earlier, went to a small-time rural school and started with a B.Sc degree from Andhra University; Dhirubhai Ambani did not even go to college; G.R. Gopinath, who changed the face of the Indian aviation industry, graduated from the National Defence Academy; Karsanbhai Patel of Nirma fame, who took on the might of Hindustan Lever in the detergents market, had but a mere bachelor's degree in chemistry; Ela Bhatt, the lady who has changed the life of millions of women in the country though her organization, SEWA, went to Sarvajanik Girls High School in Surat, got her B.A from M. T. B. College in Surat and her law degree from Sir L. A. Shah Law College in Ahmedabad. The only thing Ivy League in the lives of these individuals is the work they carved out for themselves. One could go on, but the point has been made, one hopes.

Malcolm Gladwell, in *Outliers* (Allen Lane, 2008) supports a similar view. He provides a list of universities that the last twenty-five American Nobel laureates in medicine went to. These include Antioch College, Brown University, Depauw University, University of Notre Dame, Union College (Kentucky), Holy Cross, Gettysburg College, Hunter College, University of Washington, University of Illinois, University of Texas, and Hamilton College. These are all good institutions, but certainly not among the very top.

Similarly, he provides a list of the institutions that the last twenty-five Nobel laureates in chemistry went to. These include City College of New York (two of them), University of Dayton (Ohio), Rollins College (Florida), Grinnell College, Ohio Wesleyan University, Rice University, Hope College, Brigham Young University, University of Toronto, University of Nebraska, Dartmouth College, Berea College, Augsburg College, University of Massachusetts, Washington State University and University of Florida. Again, they may be good universities, all of them, but certainly not among the very top.

Clearly, if our child does not study at a top-level institution, not much is lost. If 60 to 70 per cent of Nobel laureates did not go to these institutions, surely there is hope for us too.

The point is that hard work, endurance, innate intelligence, initiative, perseverance, holistic development, curiosity, ability to ask questions and seek answers, people skills, intuition, balanced parenting, incentives, disincentives often far more than make up for lack of a degree from a top-notch institution. The incremental effect of a top school on one's career is bound to be marginal at best.

Unfortunately, there are no formal studies that track the performance of the students who just missed making it to the top institutions in comparison with those who did make it. Such a study might prove the point we are trying to make. But in the absence of such studies, it appears safe to say that people like Narayana Murthy, G.M. Rao or Anji Reddy may well be the examples that prove that if you are fundamentally good, well rounded and focused, perhaps the engineering or business school you went to becomes less relevant. This is exactly what we found with those Nobel laureates in physics and chemistry.

In sum, human life is long and time is a great leveller. Like water, given time, ability finds its own level. All-round development provides a far better head start in life than a top school or college by itself.

RUBBISH. AN IVY LEAGUE SCHOOL DOES MATTER

That may well be your reaction to my assertion. If a good start really does not matter so much, why do millions of parents strain hard to get their wards admission into this or that school? Why do millions of students work overtime with coaching classes for preparing for the entrance examinations to national level institutions? Surely no one can deny that a top-class degree starts off a youngster on the path to a good life? So why am I advising parents not to worry about getting their children admission in good institutions? How can one say that parents should not or need not exhort their children towards better performance in their studies or in national entrance tests? Even if a good start does not matter for a very bright child, surely it must matter for most average children? Surely admission into a good school, college or institution is a ticket to a good life?

If that's your contention, let me clarify. I am not saying that a good school does not matter. It does. It is simply that according to me, a good start in life is not all about the best possible school, or best possible college or any other institution of excellence. Of course, it will be nice if our child did manage to get admission into one of those. Of course it gets your child well on his way to a good beginning. But to my mind, a good start in life is as much, or more about, a youngster's overall development; it is about developing in the youngster a sense of curiosity, about learning to learn, about developing a team spirit, about having a keen interest to read, and about cooperation as much as competition. So you see it is not a good start that I am calling unimportant; it is a particular definition of good start that I am questioning.

I am also saying that depriving your child of his childhood by making him work fourteen-hour days; putting his nose to the grindstone to prepare for entry into one of those institutions of excellence; filling up the child with a sense of failure if he does not make it; subjecting the child to extreme stress through your own huge expectations; and generally by cramming his calendar even as he is still cutting his milk teeth, you might be taking away from your child a lot more than what you might be giving him in the way of a 'good start'. What I am saying is that the wrong kind of 'good start' can take away the childhood from the child.

Alfred Binet, the renowned nineteenth-century French psychologist, observed over a hundred years ago, 'It's not always the people who start out the smartest who end up the smartest.'

If you look around, you will find any number of bright youngsters who started off from modest schools and colleges, got their MBAs from not necessarily the best business schools, but were so well rounded that after some three to four years of work experience, made it to some outstanding careers. If you take a look at where they are today, I would wager that most such candidates are likely to be ahead of the sprinters of comparable background and age in their careers.

I am, of course, not trying to say that sprinters are always, or for that matter often, losers in life as compared to long-distance runners. All I am trying to say is that one can be a winner, and what is more, enjoy life in general and childhood in particular, as a long-distance runner more than one can as a 100-metre sprinter. What I am saying is that sprinters rarely ever finish first in a marathon. What I am also saying is that as parents, we frequently think that the lack of 100-metre-dash qualities in a child is a 'missing success chip' and start giving the child all the wrong signals – knowingly or unknowingly, directly or indirectly, overtly or covertly – as if the child is destined to be a failure. Parents frequently show much more overt affection to a child achieving 95 per cent than one getting 65 per cent in the school tests, for example, completely ignoring the overall context of life.

OPPORTUNITIES EVERYWHERE

Most sprint coach parents forget that while life in India today has indeed become extremely 'competitive', the opportunities have risen manifold as well. While the population may have doubled in the last thirty-five-odd years, making our world appear more competitive, the fact is that today, job opportunities have probably grown by an order of magnitude, that is, some ten times.

Just think about the time when you (the parent of a teenaged kid) were a teenager yourself.

How many airlines operated in the country then – two? How many airlines operate today in the country, with each airline needing its share of CEOs, pilots, maintenance and flight engineers, front desk staff, back office staff, marketing staff, on-flight staff, logistics staff, catering staff, and so forth, not to mention the need for professionals in the related industries such as more travel agents, transporters, etc., etc. – Eight? Ten?

How many software firms were there to employ you when you were graduating – Two? Three? How many of them are there today – 100? 500?

How many auto companies were there to employ you in your time? Hindustan Motors and Premier Automobiles? And today?

Were there any BPOs and call centres then? Or mutual funds? Or venture capitalists?

Or corporate stock market brokers? Or stock market regulators? Or private road operators? Or private airports?

Or could you start up your own firm in a garage and hope to succeed?

Could you be a chef and a celebrity at the same time?

Or a jewellery designer? Or run an art gallery? Or run a gym?...

Do you know that in 2006-07 alone 90 pharmacy colleges, 69 engineering colleges and 52 other institutions of higher learning were added, excluding medical/dental colleges? At the time of writing this chapter, about 24,000 seats were being added in MBA, MCA and BE courses in the country annually by the All India Council for Technical Education. On an average at least 50 MBA institutions are being added annually in the country in recent years. Compare this with less than fifteen institutions in all granting business management degrees in the country until 1970. In 2007-08 over 250 engineering colleges were added in the country. These increases alone are way more than the total number of seats that existed in the 1960s and 1970s when I, and presumably you (if you are the parent of a college-going kid), were in school.

Do you recall thirty years ago what a big deal it used to be to get into an engineering or a medical college? Today at least the private engineering and medical colleges come to your doorstep offering seats to your kid. 'Oh, these aren't the top engineering or medical colleges,' you might say. But honestly, tell me, do you know which medical college your physician graduated from? Or your dentist, for that matter? Or your heart specialist? You go to your doctor or heart specialist or dental surgeon because he or she is good at what he does, not the college he or she went to. The point is, no matter which institution your kid graduates from, if he is fundamentally well prepared for life, he is bound to do well. The business or medical school he goes to will get him his first job. But the second job onwards he will be on his own.

In response to a question about what he looks for in professionals, Warren Buffett is once known to have answered, 'I don't look for the usual credentials such as an MBA, a pedigree (Harvard, Wharton), or cash reserves or market cap of their firm. What I look for is just a passion in their eyes; I think that's the key. A person who is hungry will always do well.' And these are not attitudes taught in a business school. Nor is this value taught to a child who is forced to perform against his will and interest. Passion is an attribute that is best taught by giving the child space to do whatever he likes.

While the competition has only doubled in the last thirty-five years or so (with doubling of the population), career opportunities have probably gone up ten to fifteen times. Under the circumstances, the tremendous pressure we exert upon our kids to sprint does seem quite misplaced, not to mention the umpteen personality disorders or even suicidal tendencies such parental pressures can crank up.

There are any number of websites that give you amazing number of possibilities as career choices for any given educational background. For example, the website of the University of Adelaide provides umpteen options for science graduates.[5] Similarly, the K-State's (Kansas) website provides scores of career options for any given educational background.[6] Most of these career options are also available in India.

So then, what should be your parenting like, with respect to performance-related pressures?

IF YOUR CHILD IS A SPRINTER

If your kid is a natural sprinter, it may well be that you are proud that your kid is topping his class year after year, and in addition captaining the school cricket team and the tennis team. Well, good for you and for the kid, particularly if the kid is doing it all without burning himself up prematurely. But if you are exhorting him to top every exam and captain every sport camp, and attend all possible hobby clubs, well, you may be making the light of your life burn at both ends and in all probability curbing his healthy development.

---

[5] http://www.sciences.adelaide.edu.au/future/prerequisite_info. pdf (Last accessed on 8 January 2010.)

[6] http://www.k-state.edu/acic/majorin/ (Last accessed on 8 January 2010.)

Asking their kids to try harder comes naturally to all parents. But how many of us can tell our hard-sprinting kid to take it easy? How many of us ever tell our child that it's not at all necessary that one push unnaturally hard to outdo other kids? Competition with others, like in a long-distance or cross-country run, should be reserved for much later in life, when one is probably better equipped to handle it. If one does not learn the values of cooperation, sharing and giving when one is a kid, it's unlikely that one will ever pick up those values.

There is certainly nothing wrong for a kid to be in an occasional spurt of intense competition with other kids, much as in a long-distance run, a runner may suddenly decide not to let anyone get ahead of him at least till that next culvert. But that kind of competition is still within the framework of running the long race and not winning the short dash. There is so much potential in most of us that excelling oneself is more often than not far more rewarding, far more satisfying and in fact takes one much further in life than competing against others. Competing with others is more often than not a recipe for dissatisfaction, jealousy and hence unhappiness.

IF YOUR KID IS A CROSS-COUNTRY RUNNER

If your kid is a natural long-distance runner, your job is largely simplified – all you have to do is just let him be, more or less. You just help the kid acquire more of the long-distance runner's qualities. If on his own steam, the child occasionally shows the sprinter's keenness and impatience to outperform those around him, that should be fine. Just let the kid be, as long as that competitiveness does not turn to dismay or acute unhappiness at failure, and come at the expense of the more desirable qualities of a long-term performer. For example, he might be distraught at having got a particular sum wrong in an exam by some oversight, even though he knew how to answer it correctly. What do you do? If you express equal dismay at the mistake, or directly berate him for the oversight or the lack of concentration, you are effectively being a sprint coach once again. What you should probably do is to tell him that this little error on his part is no different from a marathon runner tripping somewhere early on his 42 km track – it's hardly going to make a difference to the outcome of the race. What is important is to learn from what went wrong and try not to repeat the mistake.

IT'S NOT ALWAYS ONE OR THE OTHER

Of course, in real life, no one is ever a pure this or pure that. Often, one may take it easy for years and then suddenly make a resolution to do well or top or score in one or the other area. A child may not have shown a great deal of interest in academics per se. But it is not unusual for such a child to excel in a particular field, a particular subject or a particular examination, when the child takes it upon himself to do so. Such a switch between bouts of sprints and jogs is quite natural and should be accepted in a healthy spirit. The trick is not to pressurize the children into this or that, but let him get interested in a variety of things, and grow holistically by avoiding over-parenting, over-schooling and over-tutoring.

ANYBODY MAY CREATE OPPORTUNITIES

There is this inspiring little story narrated to me by Kishore Mahbubani, the former ambassador of Singapore to the United Nations, and presently a Professor in the National University of Singapore. Mahbubani was e-introduced to me by N.R. Narayana Murthy. The story, that of Ms Dai from Xian, as sent to me by Mahbubani, is:

Ms Dai came to Singapore in the mid-1990s to learn English. To help her pay her way through school, she gave tuitions in Chinese. My wife, Anne, and I employed her. She taught our three children well.

After Singapore, she returned to Xian and set up an English Language school. Initially, it was a very small operation. However, by the time we visited her in 2002, the small school had grown. It had a few thousand students and the campus had many buildings. She also had a fleet of Mercedes-Benz cars. In short, in less than a decade, she went from being a tuition teacher employed by us to becoming an entrepreneur who could employ me instead.

The story of Ms Dai illustrates how fast China is growing.

Now what else does that story tell us? That one does not have to have a great start to do well in life. Entrepreneurship, initiative, the desire to persevere, convert opportunities to realities, dream even as you are on the move – these are not qualities that one learns by blindly running the rat race in schools and colleges. For developing such attributes, one needs to mould a child to take a long-term view of life.

In my own life, I have seen different boys who used to come to clean our cars. A simple task one might think. True, there were those who considered it a simple task. They would take a mop cloth and a bucket of water and clean the car mechanically. On the other hand, there were those who would tell you if one of the tyres had a flat, or if oil had leaked from the engine or if a new scratch or dent had been spotted. They defined their job more broadly and stretched a little more. At least one of them, I recall, was so much in demand that he was beginning to command a slight premium from the car owners in the apartment block. He would informally employ a couple of other boys, whom he would pay the standard rate to clean the cars, oversee their work and pocket the premium. He was a budding entrepreneur.

Along similar lines, I came across this delightful story through the usual forwards on my gmail. The story, that goes under the title, 'Ducks Quack, Eagles Fly', is attributed to Harvey Mackay.[7]

According to the story, Harvey Mackay was waiting in line with a friend for a ride at the airport. When a cab pulled up, Harvey noticed that the car was gleaming and the driver very smartly turned out. The driver politely introduced himself as Wally, and opened the passenger door for Harvey and handed a card containing his mission statement, which was:

> To get my customers to their destination in the quickest, safest and cheapest way possible, in a friendly environment.

---

[7] The author of the bestsellers *Swim with the Sharks without Being Eaten Alive* and *Beware the Naked Man Who Offers You His Shirt*. However, the exact source of the story is unavailable.

Apparently Harvey was still reeling under the shock of a cabbie with a mission statement when he noticed that the cab was as clean inside as it was on the outside. And then, Wally offered him a choice of coffee and cold drinks and a set of news papers and magazines to read.

As they were pulling away, Wally handed him another card containing the list of radio stations and the music they played. He also offered to set the air-conditioning at a preferred temperature and then advised Harvey of the best route to his destination for that time of day. He also let him know that he'd be happy to chat and tell him about some of the sights on the way or, if Harvey preferred, leave him alone with his thoughts.

Amazed at all this, Harvey wanted to know if Wally, the driver, had always been like that.

Wally replied in the negative, saying that until a couple of years ago, his cab had been dowdy as any cab. He complained just as loudly about every conceivable thing as anybody else. And then one day he heard the personal growth guru, Wayne Dyer, on the radio. Apparently Wayne urged the listeners to stop complaining and to differentiate themselves from competition. 'Don't be a duck. Be an eagle. Ducks quack and complain. Eagles soar above the crowd,' was his message.

From then on Wally decided to be a soaring eagle instead of a quacking duck!

The difference between quacking and soaring was that while other cabbies drove yellow cabs, Wally was offering a limo service out of a Yellow Cab!

Well, I don't know if this story belongs here. Maybe it does, maybe it does not. But what Wally learnt and practised is not what any school teaches you. But that is something a parent can certainly impart to a child. To me that is the import of the story.

Perhaps this is the reason why, according to the eighteenth-nineteenth century British essayist William Hazlitt, 'The world judges of men by their ability in their professions, and we judge of ourselves by the same test; for it is on that on which our success in life depends.'[8] Hazlitt does not mention which profession. I am sure he meant any profession. Excellence is the key; not the profession. I have actually seen a street cleaner in Switzerland and another one in China use his pocket knife to scrape the edge of the pavement before sweeping it clean. I would any day be one of those cleaners who take pride in keeping the pavement under their charge scrupulously clean, or the gardener who keeps the best garden patch in the city, than an inefficient corporate honcho. That is the long and short of it.

Recall once again Anna Pavlova's words that success lies in the satisfaction of accomplishment, whatever that accomplishment may be.

> *But not everybody is accomplished enough to think consciously of being successful. Isn't there a whole world out there that just takes life as it comes? What should be their attitude to life?*

---

8   William Hazlitt, *Characteristics; in the Manner of Rochefoucauld's Maxims* (1823).

6 CAN ORDINARY WALKERS JOG?

*I don't make deals for the money. I've got enough, much
more than I'll ever need. I do it to do it.*

—DONALD TRUMP

THE WORLD IS FULL OF ORDINARY PEOPLE WHO JUST
take life as it comes. Most of us may not have begun with
any fancy start in life. We may be into our middle age, but do
not believe we have achieved anything significant. Leave alone
sprint, we may just be ambling along in life. It may be that
our life is neither a success nor a failure. It's just an average
life. So much so, we may believe that life has passed us by.
Having missed a great start in life and having been 'in the rut'
too long, we believe and behave as if life has slipped through
our fingers – like sand through an hourglass.

If ours is one such life, what sense do the previous chapters
make? With no great start in life, into middle age, close to
retirement and an average career behind us, what sprint or
marathon are we referring to?

I am going to give you a number of examples of people
whom in my professional life I have had occasion to get
to know or know of. Yes, they were ambling along for a

considerable stretch of their life, and found their inspiration or calling a little late in life. But they did not let that dampen their spirits. They created a second chance for themselves, a second career, if you will – a career that was far more meaningful than their earlier ones and which gave them a higher sense of fulfilment – the kind of fulfilment that few of us ever find. They certainly didn't do it for money. Nor did they do it for fame. They did it to do it!

MANI AND SOCARE

Take V. Mani, a retired Assistant General Manager of the Reserve Bank of India, Bangalore, for example. An average career with neither too many highs nor too many lows, one might say, and one would not be terribly wrong. Was he running a sprint? Certainly not. Was he even running a marathon? Difficult to say. Is life over at retirement? For some, perhaps. For others, it may continue along the path of enjoying the leisure and spending time with their grandchildren.

But in the case of Mani, the daily sight of the city prison, which he must have passed on his way to work from Rajaji Nagar to the bank every day, had pulled at his heart strings. The sight of all those children of life convicts hanging around the gates of the prison raised a million questions in his heart. To him, the answer to all these questions was only one – do something about it. So he decided to do something about it, now that he was to have all the time on hand. He took these children into his own home to look after them. He spent his retirement benefits and life's savings to set up SOCARE, or Society's Care for the Indigent, in 1999. Gradually the number of these children has grown, leading 'Mani Uncle' to set up two homes, one for boys and one for girls.

Mani and his wife Saroji play the parental role for these children. Their role is not easy. It is not just about providing food, shelter and education for these children. A child under their care might have witnessed his father murdering his mother. The father would now be in prison. The child continues to have nightmares and even at eleven, wets the bed. The Manis provide the children the love, affection, psychological security and support required to prevent these children from disintegrating from the stress of their trauma. The children are educated in some of the best schools in the surroundings. The Manis visit the schools regularly to ensure that 'their children' are not harassed by other kids for their background. The children are also supported to develop their cultural skills like singing and dancing, and technical skills, for instance working on computers. In short, the Manis are giving the children a childhood that they had nearly missed out on.

SUBASH AND ANUBHAV

Much of Subash Bose's childhood was spent on the streets. His was one of the millions of Kolkata's poorest of the poor families. Faced with acute deprivation in a family of three siblings and an ailing mother, Subash quit formal schooling at eleven. Instead, he took to the railway platforms of Howrah and Sealdah in search of a livelihood. Not making much of a living there, he hopped a train to Delhi in search of more promising pastures. He worked on the platforms on odd jobs and as domestic help as and when opportunities came his way.

In short, he went through all the kaleidoscopic experiences ranging from distress to excitement expected of a child reared on the streets. There were the police beatings and the drug abuse. There were those hungry days and hungry nights; the blistering hot summers and cold winters; sleeping on the footpath and the benches – the works. To say Subash had a challenging childhood would be an understatement.

Often we find our epiphany when we come across an individual who touches our core. Subash's core was touched by a philanthropist couple – the Jacobs. The Jacobs took young Subash under their wing and taught him to read at home. And Subash proved to be a keen learner. He was greatly influenced by Mahatma Gandhi's *My Experiments with Truth,* Rabindra Nath Tagore's *Nauka Dubi* (The Boat Sinks) and his well-known song, *Jodi tor dak shune keu na ashe tôbe êkla chôlo re* (If they answer not to thy call, walk alone), often shortened to, *ekla chalo re* (walk alone). This was his moment of awakening.

He wanted to make a difference to the world, particularly the world of the most vulnerable of the society. What were his strengths? He understood the world of street children. Upon this knowledge, that was his one strength, he decided to build his remaining life. He worked with various NGOs helping street children in Delhi. He came in contact with the railway police and other officials once again – but this time in a different role. He also made contact with a host of other officials, donors, systems, processes, volunteers, street children, etc. This provided the necessary platform for him to found Anubhav. Today, Anubhav reaches out to about 800 runaway and street children in Delhi and Haryana.

Whatever he had to make of his life, it had to be built on the one strength he identified in himself! Could he help other street children so that they wouldn't have as rough a ride of that life as he had had? He figured out that if he was to help other such children, he would have to resort to an early intervention strategy – that is, identify runaway children arriving in Delhi as early as possible and rehabilitate them.

Anubhav, founded in the early 1990s, operates rehabilitation centres for street children. He visits Delhi railway stations every day to spot runaway children. He has to spot them early if he is to beat drug and child-labour traffickers or older runaway children from identifying them before him! He spots them and provides them shelter at Anubhav's rehabilitation homes.

Today, Subash Bose runs a practical rehabilitation programme – drop-in and night shelter – that offers a wash, a dinner and a bed, and that takes care of about 200 runaway children coming to Delhi every year. His shelter near the Delhi Cantonment Station also provides some outreach at other railway stations. Through Anubhav, Subash offers every street child a chance in life – a chance for protection, a chance for family reunification, a chance for education, recreation, health and development, and thus a chance to a sense of entitlement in life.

RAJA AND NEW ARK MISSION

Chances are the name of Auto Raja in Bangalore would ring several bells in some quarters. The son of a telephone linesman, Auto Raja, having run away from home, was a child of the streets and took to stealing, gambling and drinking rather early in life. He led the life of a vagabond, eating and sleeping amidst the mongrels on the streets of Bangalore for nearly two years. He tried his hand at various jobs, including driving auto rickshaws and taxis to working as a bouncer for a while with the auto rickshaw union. It was while driving his auto rickshaw and witnessing life's myriad miseries from close quarters on the streets of Bangalore that Auto Raja had his epiphany. The realization that he had but one life and it was up to him to make something of it took root.

From that moment on, Auto Raja has been a 'Mother Teresa' of sorts for Bangalore's wretched. He resolved to take care of the dying and the destitute of the streets and set up the New Ark Mission. The mission is a godsend for the destitute and the dying. Today, T. Raja is joined by his wife and three children on the mission. In the last thirteen years, their mission has rescued over 3,000 people from the streets of Bangalore, of whom 1,300 died a peaceful death, loved and cared for, and 700 were reunited with their families! Would you say Auto Raja is leading a successful life? Surely to be successful in life, there are no prerequisites, no good starts and no constraints, other than your own will.

KISHORE AND KARUNASHRYA

A Google search on Kishore S. Rao will not throw up the name as a former chief executive or head of any major corporate. But the search would certainly throw up a number of hits on an organization called Karunashrya. Retiring after thirty-five long years in the corporate sector, Kishore Rao set up Karunashrya in 1994 – a hospice or a rest home facility for advanced cancer patients in Bangalore. His focus has been on alleviating pain and providing support to terminally ill cancer patients. These are typically patients who might have been discharged from overcrowded hospitals because no more treatment was possible. Karunashrya helps them die with dignity, completely free of charge, and even caters to such patients in their own homes.

Kishore Rao is a living example that anyone with passion and compassion can be a change agent. Even though he is not a medical practitioner, with little or no exposure to the NGO sector or for that matter to cancer-related matters, he managed to set-up Karunashrya, which has extended its care and support to about 10,000 cancer patients since its inception. If you walk (not sprint!) into the serene campus of Karunashraya, seeing the tranquillity there you will not realize that on an average one patient dies in the hospice every day, or that the fifty-odd patients you see there may be left with less than one month of life.

Kishore Rao has used his last leg of professional life to silently extend palliative care to the most wretched and the underprivileged sections of society, a great majority of whom might otherwise have died suffering intolerable pain and abject poverty.

MAHANTESH AND SAMARTHAN TRUST FOR THE DISABLED

Mahantesh G. Kivadasannavar is the harbinger of hope and smiles for hundreds and thousands of physically challenged children and adults in southern India. Mahantesh is 100 per cent visually challenged himself and has known the hardships that accompany one so challenged. Mahantesh did not let his visual challenge come in the way of his education, and with grit and determination started an organization called Samarthanam Trust for the Disabled in Bangalore. He has been working relentlessly to help the lives of others who are physically challenged. He offers a range of educational and life-skill oriented programmes to children with disabilities, particularly those from weaker socio-economic sections, with a view to nurturing their skills and talent. His goal has been to ensure that these children will overcome all prejudices, shed all inhibitions and excel in life.

People interacting with Mahantesh hardly suspect his visual impairment. Such is the power of his other four faculties that he has brought into play, that he behaves like one who can see the world and people. He enjoys playing cricket and is quite up on all the key developments in the world and never misses a chance to relate with people and encourage them to join his mission of supporting the physically challenged.

ASHISH GOYAL

Not everyone has to run an NGO to qualify in this chapter! Take Ashish Goyal, for example. Ashish was just another undergraduate – one of thousands, who passed their B.Com from one of the hundreds of colleges in Mumbai - but was good enough to get into SP Jain Institute of Management – a good business school, but not what you would count as the absolute best. He secured second rank in his MBA programme – a good achievement, one might say, but nothing extraordinary. In fact when it came to campus placement, he was never shortlisted by any of the major corporates that visited the campus, though Ashish always performed extremely well. He was one those few who were left without a job, when most others had been placed.

He was nearing despair when once again, he happened to top the written test of one of the banks that came for a campus placement. Looking at his performance in the test and then his performance in the interview, he was selected as a management trainee in the treasury. In the next five years, young Ashish did exceedingly well and was finally placed in Mumbai to market derivative instruments for the bank's treasury. Ashish did this with élan once again and that's when he took his GMAT (Graduate Management Aptitude Test) and scored a scorching 760 out of 800 that placed him in the top 99++ percentile. That is, he was adjudged better than 99.99 per cent of the comparable global population taking the test. This got him entry into the Wharton School of Management for another MBA. And two years later he passed out with the President's commendation, that is, somewhere at the top of the batch. He then went on to take up an investment banking job with one of the world's leading investment banking firms.

None of the above is remarkable – until one is told that Ashish started going blind at the age of ten or so, and by nineteen he was nearly totally blind, and 100 per cent blind by 21! Ashish uses a synthesizer linked to his computer so that he can hear a verbal description of the contents of the screen. Ashish perfected his skills so thoroughly in the bank when he was in the treasury department, spending hours before a Reuter's screen, that he could 'read' the screen better than any visually normal person. Clearly Ashish used his mind, his willpower and his other four faculties to more than make up for the gradual loss of the crucial fifth one. He did not waste too much time on self-pity and realized that he had to play the game of life with the cards fate had dealt him. Did Ashish have a great start in life? You are the best judge. He virtually had to re-learn and redo things even as he was going blind during his teens – in some ways the best years in one's life. But Ashish leads a full life – there are few cricket matches that he does not see. He finds New York beautiful. He lives his life larger than most of us do.

So how do we instil such values in our children?

7 LET CHILDREN GROW IN THEIR OWN TIME

Early one morning, a mother went to wake up her son.
'Wake up, son. It's time to go to school!'
'But why, Mom? I don't want to go.'
'Give me two reasons why you don't want to go.'
'Well, the kids hate me for one, and the teachers hate me, too!'
'Oh, that's no reason not to go to school. Come on now and get ready.'
'Give me two reasons why I should go to school.'
'Well, for one, you're 52 years old. And for another, you're the Principal!'

—ANONYMOUS

ATHLETES FORCING THEIR PACE UNNATURALLY THROUGH long runs are known to have had cardiac arrests mid-course. It's the same with kids who are driven to run a sprint under acute pressure from parents for performance. According to some surveys in Delhi, about 70 per cent of schoolgoing children suffer from stress and 80 per cent of all suicides among children are related to parental pressures for performance in school. In fact so widespread is this phenomenon that the Central Board of Secondary Education (CBSE) issued renewed instructions to schools to do away with examinations altogether up to Class V.[1] And now, parliament is all set to discuss whether examinations should be done away with right up to Class X. The CBSE has also been working towards doing away with the term 'fail' altogether and replacing it with alternative terms such as 'unsatisfactory', 'repeat', or providing letter grades such as A, B, C and D, since the stigma of 'failure' is psychologically devastating to a young mind (September 2007). In fact, as early as 2004, the board had asked all CBSE schools to replace the pass-fail criteria with continuous evaluation system up to Standard V, though the schools in their wisdom are yet to comply with that requirement.

The CBSE's concern with examinations is understandable. Come annual exam-season, we see a spate of suicides by children reported in the local press. Children suffering from acute or suicidal depression are often driven to it as a result of overparenting, and parental pressures and expectations. Here is a small sample of what some children have to say about the examination pressure they face (posted on ndtv.com, 12 August 2009):

'We have to stay at home. The build-up to this stress is all through the year. You're told you are a board exam class and you need to study.'

'We are so pressurized. We have to crack the competitive exams and also get above 90 per cent in the board exams to get into a good college. These pills at least make you feel that if

---

[1] *Indian Express*, 18 May 2008.

you are taking them they are helping you. One feels optimistic about things, at least psychologically.'

Are we shocked about the reference to the pills?

Elsewhere, observes ndtv.com, 'As the students find themselves in the midst of board exams, the pressure levels seem to be reaching a feverish pitch. The endless study hours, the bulk of syllabus; the overwhelming pressure of parents and peers is wreaking havoc on the students' psyche.

'What was once meant to be a stepping stone to higher education has now almost degenerated to being representative of the most stressful period of a student's life.

'Suicides and other extreme measures are becoming more of a norm than an exception. Six students have already committed suicide while 300 have attempted it.'

Says Dr H.S. Dhavale of Nair Hospital in Mumbai, commenting on the mental health of adolescent girls in Arogya.com, 'Because of parental pressure and unhealthy competition, career-choosing is becoming a real problem. Many parents try to force a career on their children even if they don't have aptitude for the same, which may disturb their mental health.'

So you see, while the reasons for parental pressures may vary, the fact remains that parental pressure to sprint when the kid ought to be running a steady pace is highly dysfunctional.

In fact, often parental pressure is not merely about the child. It also has to do with the parents' own unfulfilled desires and ambitions, which they expect to realize vicariously through their children – the parents who wanted to get into the top institutions, or those who wanted to become doctors, architects or civil servants in their time, and for whatever reasons didn't or couldn't. So now they want their child to realize their dreams for them. Given their relative present affluence, they flog the child from one tuition class to another and from one coaching class to another.

The phenomenon we are focusing upon is universal, even if to varying degrees, whatever may be the reasons underlying parental pressures.

For example, consider the scene in the US: Dr Michelle Miller and Dr Edward Day teaching at the Pennsylvania State University observe in the university's website, based on a study carried out at Altoona Campus, 'College women most vulnerable to suicidal thoughts are those with mothers who not only require stellar performance in school but keep raising the bar of expectation.' Again, in another study in 2002, the two draw a similar conclusion.[2]

Screams a headline in the *San Francisco Chronicle* (8 May 2005), 'Experts recommend moderation for students who face intense parental pressures to excel'. The report begins thus:

> As the boy played behind the bushes at his Redwood City school, his obviously agitated mother grabbed him, abruptly escorting him to her car.
>
> 'She asked him what he thought he was doing and proceeded to tell him all in one breath that he would never get into a good university or have a good job if he spent all his

---

[2]   Michelle Miller and L. Edward Day, 'Family Communication, Maternal and Paternal Expectations, and College Students' Suicidality', *Journal of Family Communication*, Volume 2, Issue 4, 2002.

time playing and goofing around,' said Jim Dassise, a parent who watched the episode unfold. [According to the mother], 'He should be more like one of his friends, who spent his time studying and having good grades.'

The boy was about 9 years old.

Sounds familiar?

The *Chronicle* also quotes a Stanford School of Education Lecturer and the founder of 'Stressed Out Students' (SOS), Denise Pope, saying, 'the real parental pressure is for grades, not knowledge, so sometimes cheating is the simplest path. Teachers cheat too, inflating grades because it's easier than fighting with parents.'

TRAINING THE CHILD OR STRAINING THE CHILD?

A number of educationists and thinkers have expressed concern over the years about the pressures on modern-day children from relentless early-school testing. Rowan Williams, the Archbishop of Canterbury, wonders if society was right to 'put such an emphasis on testing from such an early age and give that such prominence at a time when it seems to undermine children's confidence and increase their levels of pressure'.[3] Well, the good Archbishop spoke in the context of the UK, but he might as well have spoken for kids in India, or for that matter, kids anywhere.

Worldwide, children are being diagnosed with increasing incidence of high blood pressure. There are research results

---

[3]   *Guardian*, 18 September 2006.

that correlate stress with high blood pressure among the very young.

Of course, stress is a part of the growing-up process, but parents need to ensure that the stress is not such as to undermine a child's physical or psychological health.

How do you know if your child is stressed? You may want to look out for the following symptoms[4]:

- The child develops physical symptoms, like headaches and stomach pains.
- The child seems restless, tired, and agitated.
- The child appears depressed and will not communicate how he or she feels.
- The child seems less interested in an activity that was once very important to him or her, such as baseball or dance class.
- The child's grades begin to fall, and he or she has less interest than usual in attending classes and doing homework.
- The child exhibits antisocial behavior, such as lying and stealing, forgets or refuses to do chores, and seems more dependent on the parent than in the past.
- Other common symptoms induced by excessive stress not included in the list above may be, a child's refusal to go to school; obesity; migraine; diabetes; secretiveness and so forth.

---

[4]   From Ohio State University Extension Fact Sheet.

In fact, a study in Ireland also shows that parental pressure on children is making them grow up faster than the generation before! This may be understandable. How many parents today have the time to read bedtime stories to their children? For that matter, how many children really have the time to read fairy tales today? Where is the time for fantasy and make-believe? Today, even a four-year-old urban child will tell you with a straight face that there are no ghosts or fairies or that there is no Santa, while in yester years, we probably looked for a *vetal* on the tamarind tree or mermaids in the sea when we were, say, nine.

Again, all this is hardly surprising, given that today's kids have to organize their time and structure their activities far more closely than most executives of the earlier generation. Such pressure on time, pressure on performance, and pressure on reading for competitive advantage, rather than out of interest and for self-improvement, is probably taking its toll on children in terms of the quality of childhood time.

EFFECTS OF PARENTS' VALUES ON CHILDREN

We would all agree that parents play a significant role in the achievements of their children. But do high-aspiring parents put too much pressure on their children to perform at unrealistically high levels? Are the parents trying to satisfy their own needs in the process? Is such pressure detrimental to the high-achieving children? Do parents of overachieving kids commence their pressures too early in their children's lives?

Research at Johns Hopkins finds that the answer to practically all these questions is in the affirmative.[5]

Are we not really cheating the kids out of their childhood today and laying the foundation for an unhealthy society for tomorrow?

Now what do you think a renowned sprinter (yes, a sprinter) has to say about the parenting style of today? Let us hear Ashwini Datta (formerly Ashwini Nachappa) on that.

But first, let us get to know Ashwini a little better. She is an Olympian, Asian and a National top athlete, who excelled in 100-, 200- and 400-metre sprints, and reigned over the women's field and track events around the turn of the 1980s and held sway until 1992. Following an injury, she chose to retire from track and field at her peak, and withdrew her Olympics nomination.

She was one of the fastest Indian runners. She came from an average middle class family. She did her early schooling in Kolkata (then Calcutta) in Bengali medium. While her father continued to work in Calcutta, she, her mother and an older sister moved to Bangalore in 1975, when she was about eight. With two establishments to run on a single income, they managed in a single-bedroom house in which the living conditions were merely functional, sans any luxuries. The house was run on a very tight budget. It took some time and lots of running around for her mother to get the eight-year-old into a school in Bangalore. Her earlier education in Bengali medium

---

[5] Center for Talented Youth (2002b) *Parents' Values and Children's Perceived Pressure,* Topical Research Series 4, Baltimore, MD, Johns Hopkins Center for Talented Youth.

did not help her assimilation into the English-medium school. But the child wasn't going to be an Olympian for nothing, if such things as Bengali and English were going to faze her.

She made the most of the presence of Kanteerava stadium located near her house. To begin with, her mother ensured that the girls spent their evenings at Kanteerava. She was beginning to run so well even at that young age that it was only a matter of time before the late Mohinder Singh Gill – India's leading triple jumper and a 1972 Olympian – spotted her and helped her train, and she became an easy winner at school-level events. From there it was only a matter of time to scale state, national, Asian and Olympian heights. The high points in her career, apart from representing the country in the Olympics, included beating the legendary P.T. Usha, not once but twice in as many weeks, and winning the Arjuna Award.

Today, she is a multi-faceted individual, a former top athlete, a former actress, committed social worker and now an educationist. She has set up a first-rate sports academy which is predominantly aimed at giving a fair chance to children gifted in sports, alongside a sound grounding in academics.

IN ASHWINI'S OWN WORDS

On her own parenting style…

'I make sure that my children get positive reinforcements and remain positive, and stay disciplined in the sense of avoiding excesses. For giving them the required direction, I am always there. In fact I do it proactively, but never forcefully. It is important that my "pressures" are in their natural direction. At the same time, I also make sure that they devote enough time to books as well. My mandate to my kids is: As long as you manage 70 per cent marks in your school, please go ahead and pursue what gives you the maximum satisfaction.

'I believe that every child is special in some ways. The trick is to identify that specialness. If as a parent you can devote enough time to identify that specialness in your child, you just need to keep nudging the child in the right direction. Make hard work in the chosen area a way of life. Take time to guide the child in the right direction. Adversity is not necessarily bad. If you can teach a child to face adversity, the child can be allowed to take greater risks as well. It is when we shield our children from all adversity that we also make them entirely risk-averse and hence do not take chances with their special gifts and settle for safe "academic performance". Children must always be taught to compete against themselves and not with others. When I beat P.T. Usha, I consciously decided only to better my own timing and not to race against her. That way, one is always focused against self and always trying to better oneself rather than bettering others.'

On parenting today in general...

'Today, the parenting scene is taking a turn that raises many concerns. Lifestyles have changed so drastically that priorities have changed. It is important to have money to live a comfortable life, but isn't it more important to have our children grow up with care and attention and love? Parents are so busy with their own lives that many of the nuances in the growth of the child that ought to catch their attention in fact escape their notice.

'I will give you a personal example. I am not from an athletic family. Neither of my parents had anything remotely to do with athletics. Nor is my husband from an athletic or sports-oriented family. Both my husband and I are sportspeople and for us, exercise is an integral part of our lives. And every evening when we used to play a few games of badminton, my daughter, who was barely four, liked to play with the marker boy and because we made playing badminton a routine for ourselves, our daughter too got into the groove and took to the game most naturally. We encouraged her because we could see that her hand-eye coordination was very good. Once she started winning some matches, the winning became its own reinforcement and today she is doing well in the junior circuit. The point is, if a parent does not have the time or the eye to identify that special skill of the child, a wonderful opportunity might well be lost for the child.'

On the need for holistic development of children...

'Parents must realize that there is life beyond textbooks. If children are not introduced into games and sports and group activities rather early, they tend to become more self-centred and miss out on an entire dimension in life. In fact increasingly, children have little interaction outside their school environment. Most are almost never introduced to even newspapers and magazines till rather late into their teens, if then. At home they are often tied up with their cell phones, computer chats or televisions. Today, you rarely see children engaged in cycling or playing "Santolia" in the common playgrounds.[6] So where is the social interaction? Speaking for myself, I insist that my children spend a minimum of two hours outside home in the evenings, preferably in the open air, whether they are playing games, sports, or whatever.'

Ashwini is quite categorical that it is perhaps more important to be a well-rounded individual than an academically brilliant one. Overemphasis on academics at the expense of virtually all else, overprotection by parents, combined with other distractions of the times such as television, computers and cell phones, are taking their toll on the development of a child.

Ashwini gives almost the entire credit to her mother for channelling her early interests in the direction of athletics. 'Opportunities abound for all of us, such as the presence of a stadium close to one's home. But how many mothers help children take advantage of those opportunities?' seems to be Ashwini's point.

Yes, given today's reality competition is important. A child not suited to accept competition may be like a hand-reared cub being released into the jungle for survival.

But are we readying our children properly for healthy competition? Are our schools up to the task? What is the best way to do it?

---

[6] 'Santolia' is a traditional game in which seven flat pieces of concrete or stones are placed one above the other in a little tower which is targeted with a rubber ball.

8   SCHOOLING, WORK LIFE AND COMPETITION

We are students of words; we are shut up in school, and colleges, and recitation rooms, for ten or fifteen years, and come out at last with a bag of wind, a memory of words, and do not know a thing.

—RALPH WALDO EMERSON

BY NOW I AM SURE YOU ARE SOMEWHAT SCEPTICAL. IT'S all very well to talk of marathons and sprints conceptually, but in these competitive times, how can one or one's child survive without the spirit of competition? I have also encountered comments such as, 'All that is fine except when your own kid is nearing Class XII!' The scepticism is somewhat understandable; it's one of those things that the mind understands, but the heart doesn't. Where is the evidence that a kid being prepared for a so-called 'marathon' in a non-competitive environment will do better in the long term than a sprinting kid? Well, to be honest, I do not have any evidence in terms of numbers. But as an academic I have been associated with youngsters for twenty-eight years of my life. And I can cite you one good example, namely, the students passing out from the schools run by the Krishnamurti Foundation. Some of the better known ones under this umbrella are the Rishi Valley School in Chittoor District and the Valley School in Bangalore. The school's basic philosophy is to bring out the best in a child. J. Krishnamurti's philosophy of education, as reflected in the working of the schools run by the Foundation, is best expressed in his own words:

The purpose, the aim and drive of schools, is to equip the child with the most excellent technological proficiency so that the student may function with clarity and efficiency in the modern world. A far more important purpose than this is to create the right climate and environment so that the child may develop fully as a complete human being. This means giving the child the opportunity to flower in goodness so that he or she is rightly related to people, things and ideas, to the whole of life. To live is to be related. There is no right relationship to anything if there is not the right feeling for beauty, a response to nature, to music and art – a highly developed aesthetic sense.

I think it is fairly clear that competitive education and the development of the student in that process . . . are very, very destructive. We must be very clear in ourselves what we want – clear that a human being must be the total human being, not just a technological human being. If we concentrate very much on examinations, on technological information, on making the child clever, proficient in acquiring knowledge while we neglect the other side, then the child will grow up into a one-sided human being. When we talk about a total human being, we mean not only a human being with inward understanding, with a capacity to explore, to examine his or her inward state and the capacity of going beyond it, but also someone who is good in what he does outwardly. The two must go together. That is the real issue in education: to see that when the child leaves the school, he is well established in goodness, both outwardly and inwardly.

In fact the Rishi Valley School's website goes on to add:

'The intention is to awaken the intelligence of the student so that he or she may "flower in goodness". The cultivation of a global outlook, a love of nature and a concern for our fellow human beings are all part of the scheme of education.'

Some further goals of the educational philosophy of Rishi Valley School are:

- To educate students so that they are able to explore both the world and their inner being
- To inculcate a love for nature and respect for all forms of life
- To create an atmosphere of affection, order and freedom without either fear or licence
- Not to condition the students in any particular belief, either religious, political or social, so that their minds may remain free to ask fundamental questions, enquire and learn.

I suppose even if the school is achieving half of its intent, it is probably doing a very good job of preparing the children for the marathon of life.

Surely, the purpose of schools cannot be to cram the minds of students with facts – however useful; it is to inspire them to think, if that is possible, and always to think for themselves.

Schools cannot be 'the state-controlled manufactory of echoes', to borrow a phrase from British writer Norman Douglas. The Krishnamurti schools come close to this ideal.

The only additional angle I would like to add is that this environment does not have to be necessarily or exclusively provided by a school. Parents too have to take their share of responsibility to provide it or support it. Given that most schools do not necessarily endorse the pedagogical philosophy of the Krishnamurti schools, parents do have their job cut out.

How well do the students of Krishnamurti Foundation perform in today's competitive world? you may wonder. Well, at least as well as, and perhaps better than most other schooling systems, would be my answer. I personally know quite a few children who have graduated from the Rishi Valley or Valley schools and I find, on an average they are among the most complete and balanced adults of their generation that I know. Of course, while that kind of a statement may be neither here nor there, it may yet be said that these adults actually come very close to the stated philosophy of the schools' founder.

We all recognize that neither over-parenting nor over-schooling may be very healthy for a child's development. However, there is a flip side to everything. Over-parenting or over-schooling may be as tricky as under-parenting or under-schooling. Either can result in an attitude of indifference on the part of the child. For example, it is more likely that a child with a low level of self-motivation becomes further laid back in a school like the Rishi Valley, where over-instructing is not the norm. Thus, parents and schools alike need to strike the right balance and take particular caution with respect to outlying children.

But even these arguments cannot truly satisfy a parent who is aiming that his kid gets through an all-India entrance examination for engineering or medicine, for example. These entrance examinations are typically extremely competitive, with barely one per cent of the applicants getting through. Under the circumstances, they see no option but to induce, if not pressurize, the child to obtain the highest possible grades in Class XII and the entrance tests, even if it means working them like mules. After all, entrance into national institutions is an insurance against the downside in one's life.

But then, that's the very point. Assuming your kid is fundamentally bright and you do manage to condition him into clearing an important entrance exam at the cost of his overall development, you might have ensured a minimum standard for the kid in life. But you might also at the same time have capped his upward potential. You might have ensured that your kid will be ahead of most others up to the next culvert, but not necessarily be the long-distance winner.

ANOTHER LOOK AT COMPETITION

At this stage it might be useful to take another look at our view of competition. We may not be able to deny that winning a competition does provide us some happiness. That is why in most cases, happiness is not so much about how well we are doing for ourselves but about how much better we are doing in relation to others. There is considerable research that supports this view. In this context, let me ask you a question:

Would you rather that your child studying in Standard IX tops his class securing 81 per cent marks, or that he secures 92 per cent marks emerging somewhere in the top ten per cent of the class?

In other words, are you happier when your kid is *numero uno* in the peer group at a lower level of performance (81 per cent) or when he is merely in the top ten per cent of the class, but at a much higher level of performance (92 per cent)?

The question is similar to asking whether you feel happier driving a very expensive and top-end car in a town where everybody else also drives the same model, or if you would rather drive around in a somewhat less expensive mid-market brand, where everybody else drives around in an inexpensive entry-level car? As a corollary, will you be happier driving around in the mid-market car in a society where everyone else drives the top-end model, or would you rather drive around in an entry-level model where everybody else also drives the same model?

In a different analogy, are you happier when everybody in your company, including you, receives the same big salary hike (say X) or happier when everyone receives a moderate hike and you get a better-than-moderate hike but less than X? Alternatively, are you happier when nobody including you receives any salary hike, or when you receive a good hike but everyone else receives an even better hike?

Does your sense of success, happiness or satisfaction for yourself or for your child derive from relative well-being or from absolute well-being? Are you unhappy when you/ your kid are doing fairly well for yourself/himself and yet not necessarily better than your/his peers? Researchers have enough evidence to indicate that in general, those whose sense of success is internally driven are more likely to be happier than those whose sense of success is externally driven. People who want to be the best in a peer group are always in danger of being bettered by others. However, those who are their own benchmarks have less to fear on that count.

BUT ISN'T COMPETITIVENESS THE KEY TO EVERYTHING?

Don't non-competitive species go hungry and fade out? Don't non-competitive businesses go out of business? Aren't we always wishing our cricket team would outdo the competition and win every possible match? So if competition is the key to survival of the species, to success in business and most importantly, to the Indian cricket team, why isn't it equally necessary for children to be competitive? So why should schools eschew intense competition among students? In a country of 1.2 billion people, isn't life fundamentally competitive? If there are only 2,000-odd seats in a handful of coveted higher institutions with some 200,000 students vying for them, how can a child not be prepared for competition?

I am sure all those questions must have sprung to your mind, just as they did to mine. The answer is simple. To be able to prepare themselves in a changing world, children do not have to be more intelligent than others. They simply need to be more responsive to the world environment. As Charles Darwin has said, 'It is not the strongest of the species that survives, nor the most intelligent, but the one which is most responsive to change.'

We are not decrying competition at all. We are merely decrying competition as it is commonly understood in the context of children. Children, as much as species or businesses, do need to compete. But like species or businesses, more than competing against others, they need to compete essentially against themselves.

Competing against oneself is synonymous with striving for excellence. A long distance-runner competes to win the race as much as a sprinter does. However, the former runs much of the race trying to better his own previous performance. His efforts are directed inwards and not outwards. That's the kind of competition we need to advocate to schools to inculcate in kids.

As authors Farson and Keyes put it, 'Studies of high school graduates rarely find any correlation between recognition in high school and recognition thereafter... The terms are too different. What worked in high school seldom works later... Those not tested by setbacks when young, may never learn how to rebound from defeat.' In fact, they go on to add, 'Most schools do a remarkably poor job of recognizing and rewarding future achievers... The standards of success in school have very little to do with standards thereafter.'[1] Farson and Keyes are certainly not discouraging children from doing well in school; what they are saying is not to be obsessed with it.

---

[1]   Richard Farson and Ralph Keyes, *Whoever Makes the Most Mistakes Wins*, The Free Press, New York, 2002.

COMPETITION OR SCRAMBLE

It is certainly not my case that children must not be encouraged or motivated to work hard or do well at school. Nor is it my thesis that it is perfectly fine for a kid to be negligent about his school curriculum or that a kid is best left alone if we want him to realize his full potential. I am also not contending that children ought not to be made to compete. Far from it.

I do recognize that competition is very much a part of life, and cannot and ought not to be done away with, either in a child's or an adult's life. In fact we started on the premise that life is a race, albeit a marathon – and hence a competition. However, competition among children should be a more relaxed affair. It ought to be treated more lightly. It should not be a life and career issue. Competition at children's level should be for fun; not for branding kids as 'better' or 'worse'. Competition should be only motivational, and not demoralizing. It should not affect a child's perspective on larger priorities and goals in life.

Take our overcrowded educational system, for example. Even for a nursery admission in most private schools, there are often over a hundred kids 'competing' for a single seat. It is impossible to secure admission without an entrance test, though now thankfully educational authorities are coming down on the practice. But, do such competitive entrance examinations for five-year-olds have any meaning? It is extremely difficult to gain entry into national institutions, not because their standards are necessarily so high that one needs to be 1 in 100 in terms of intelligence to be able to cope with their curriculum. The 'competition' is acute because, thanks to our enormous population and the limited number of good institutions, there are a hundred students for every available seat. In fact, what we see here is not really competition. It is a scramble – a scramble for limited resources – not unlike the scramble we see when food relief reaches areas of calamity. A scramble is by no means a 'fair' process, and the most deserving are hardly the ones who necessarily end up getting the goodies.

A competition, on the other hand, unlike a scramble, ought to be a dignified contest of the deserving. Healthy competition is not merely desirable but important for a child's overall development. It helps the child gain recognition, approval and acceptance. It helps overcome weakness, helplessness and preserve individuality. And finally, it helps the child push himself harder and expand the boundaries of what he thought was possible.

Unfortunately, however, most 'competitions' we witness are not competition in this positive sense. In healthy competition, which has a moral character, individuals are able to exercise a degree of self-control and restraint in limiting or suspending the kind of aggressiveness that may be detrimental to character building. But what do we say about competition that achieves the exact opposite purpose by giving rise to negative emotions in a child? When rather than help a child overcome weakness, it engenders an inferiority complex? Or, when it leaves a child feeling a loser? Or saps the child of self-esteem and associates failure with shame rather than inspiration to superior performance?

Alas! It's this dysfunctional kind of competition that our system in general, and educational system in particular, seems to endorse.

AN INTERVIEW WITH N.R. NARAYANA MURTHY

To give you a flavour of what somebody like Narayana Murthy has to say on the attributes desirable in youngsters; what success means; academic performance versus other attributes in children; the dilemma of choices available today, etc., I bring you excerpts from my interview with the father of Indian IT industry.

Author: What attributes do you think portend 'success' in life?

NM: One who is enthusiastic, optimistic, committed, disciplined, aspirational and given to excellence in whatever he or she does. It really does not matter whether the youngster has the makings of an artist or a doctor. Without these attributes, no one ever becomes successful irrespective of the vocation chosen. Nobody can be one-dimensional and reasonably expect to be successful, whatever one's personal definition of success may be.

Author: What is your idea of success for a youngster?

NM: At the broadest level, anyone who can bring a smile on people's faces when he or she walks into a room is successful. You may bring a smile upon people's faces because of the quality of work that you do, or because of the value system that you follow or because of your commitment to society. It does not matter what you do for a living. You may be a teacher, a plumber, a soldier, a policeman, a politician, a civil servant, a businessman, a builder, or whatever – you can bring a smile to people's faces in any of these fields by teaching wonderfully, leaving the work area clean after an expert job, fighting bravely on the frontier, patrolling with diligence, serving the nation truly, being a genuine public servant, conducting business ethically, serving the community, building the nation honestly. And if you have been able to bring that smile upon people's faces, you will know you have been successful.

Author: How do you compare the importance of academic performance of growing children vis-à-vis other skills necessary in life to be successful?

NM: As I said earlier, I do not think one-dimensional skills work in the long haul in shaping a complete individual. A youngster who is purely academically bright but lacks in social and people skills, confidence, enthusiasm and discipline may get that first premium job. But to keep that job, and do well in a career, the youngster will need all those other attributes. Academic performance is just one of the attributes of success. A child who is to become a great artist or a great musician or a great mathematician or a great author requires more than just academic brilliance. Today, there are so many avenues to contribute to society and become economically well-off. One can be a successful entrepreneur whether you are an outstanding plumber, artist or a computer scientist. It is so easy to overemphasize academics at the cost of overall development of a child.

Author: What do you think hampers parents and youngsters alike, taking the wider view of success and careers?

NM: Perhaps partly it is our colonial background and partly our caste-ridden biases that make us look at some vocations as being lower than others. An average middle-class parent cannot think of their child becoming a successful plumber or a successful carpenter. But as any successful individual will tell you, all skills at the highest level become equally worthy.

Author: Do you think with increasing choices available today, a shift in the mindset of the parents and the younger generation may be happening after all?

NM: Perhaps, but rather slowly. While there is no doubt that today the younger generation has many more options than a generation ago, the mindset of parents is yet to catch up with the reality unfolding before us. Today, excellence in any field is waiting to be rewarded hugely. That is the essence of capitalism and free market. In free markets, there are no castes. The only two castes are reasonably smart, sincere, committed, and hard-working people seeking excellence in what they do on the one hand, and the idle fellows on the other hand.

Are our schools up to the task of showing the right direction to their students? If not, what is the parents' role?

9 GET INTERESTED IN READING – ANYTHING AT ALL

Circa 2050. Medical science has figured out how to package basic knowledge in pill form.

A student, needing some learning, goes to the pharmacy and asks what kind of knowledge pills are available. The pharmacist says, 'Here's a pill for English literature.'

The student takes the pill and swallows it and has new knowledge about English literature!

'What else do you have?' asks the student.

'Well, we have pills for art history, biology, and world history,' replies the pharmacist.

The student asks for these, and swallows them and has new knowledge on all those subjects. Then the student asks, 'Do you have a pill for math?'

The pharmacist says, 'Wait just a moment,' goes back into the storeroom, brings back a whopper of a pill, and plunks it on the counter.

'I have to take that huge pill for math?' inquires the student.

The pharmacist replied, 'Well, you know math always was a little hard to swallow.'

—From jokesnjokes.net[1]

Some time ago, I was invited to deliver two lectures. One was to the high school students of a very upmarket international school, and the other was to the members of a Rotary Club on career counselling from parents' perspective. In each of the lectures, a question was posed, which I think is relevant to most parents.

THE FIRST QUESTION

The first question was put up to me by the CEO of the school. The question was triggered by my advice to the students to make reading a habit – just reading, reading anything at all, reading whatever grabbed their attention. I wanted reading to become second nature to them, the idea being, if they learnt to read with more interest, comprehension and retention, the world would open up to them in all its glorious possibilities. My message was that if reading becomes a way of life, it stands one in good stead in a variety of ways. Books make wonderful friends, they help you veer away from television or other passive diversions, improve your language and communication skills, improve your world view and knowledge base in the most general sense and finally, whenever you are curious about anything at all, you learn to reach for a book to seek out

---

[1] The editor of the website claims no copyright for individual jokes on the site. In all probability the joke is in public domain.

an answer. This last – seeking answers – is perhaps the very purpose of education and the hallmark of the educated. It was also my thesis that reading, as a habit, must begin young, or else it never really becomes second nature. I am sure all of us know any number of adults who may not have read a complete book in the last ten years.

Now the question that the CEO posed to me was one which, according to him, was often posed by the children in his school. Most of these children came from very affluent backgrounds. They saw that in many cases, their parents almost never ever read. Books and reading were not part of the family culture. And yet the children found their parents in possession of every conceivable luxury in life, and 'none the worse' for not reading! In fact they were making far more money than most people, especially academics, and as far as the children could tell, they simply never read! So apparently the children would often ask their teachers:

'Why is it important to read or study when it is obvious that one can have a good life without reading?'

Surely a sad question, arising from a rather poignant state of parenting among the super-affluent, one might think. But you can empathize with that question if you put yourself in the children's shoes. Before we answer that question, we must realize that the role of the school is actually most crucial in the lives of children from the most affluent and the least affluent sections of society, even if the two sets of children go to vastly different schools. It is equally likely in either category of children that they do not witness 'average conditions' at home. In both cases, the lifestyles the children witness at home may be such that conventional role models break down.

In both cases, a balanced life may well be quite different from the conditions they observe at home. And lastly, in both cases special care and concern may be called for in the upbringing of the children which may or may not be obtained at home.

At a naïve level, the question of the CEO or his students may be answered by telling them that a habit of reading and sound education will enable them to multiply or at least keep the wealth created by their parents. One could expound on the old American saying 'from shirt sleeves to shirt sleeves in three generations' to tell the children why they must study diligently notwithstanding their affluence. But it should not take us long to realize that this question from the students is a testimony to how 'education' is understood by children today.

The message the students are getting is that education is aimed at making money. It follows then that if it is possible to make money without education or if one is inheriting enough money for a very comfortable life, where is the need for education? If such is the understanding these children have of education, then clearly the children's question is quite logical.

The children's understanding of the purpose of education can hardly be faulted. After all, isn't that the message parents, society and schools, directly or indirectly, keep reinforcing?

To answer that question, let's ask another question. Why do we, both as parents and as schools, exhort our students towards a feverish competition to score above 99 per cent marks in science subjects or drive them pell-mell to clear some select entrance exams? To ensure a good start for them, we might say. A good start to what? A good start to landing coveted jobs and careers. What are good jobs and careers, as understood by most? Jobs and careers that will pay more than other jobs and careers. After all, come March, every newspaper reinforces this understanding of education by going to town with screaming headlines on the large salaries offered to the top students in the top business schools. So then, by deductive logic, the purpose of education as we make a child see by our actions, is to find jobs that will pay more than others. Now, if a child finds that he is already very well provided for in life by his well-off parents, isn't he justified in questioning the purpose of education? That's exactly what the children in that international school had been asking the CEO.

PURPOSE OF EDUCATION

The fact is that the question asked by these children cannot be answered appropriately in a system where the very purpose of education is misunderstood. The purpose of education cannot be to find jobs. That may be an effect – a very important and desirable effect – but not the raison d'etré of education.

The basic purpose of education can only be one – to make an individual curious for knowledge, curious about anything, and instil in the individual a spirit of inquiry – asking questions, seeking answers; expanding the boundaries of his knowledge, and motivated to do so for sheer intellectual curiosity and the achievement of excellence – the hallmark of a well-rounded human being. As Einstein said, 'The important thing is not to stop questioning.' And that's what education must inculcate in a child – the habit of questioning. Education must plant ideas in the students' minds, not pour information into them.

According to Mark Lee of Krishnamurti Foundation of America[2]:

'Krishnamurti stressed the importance of discovery by both teacher and child, without coercion. This discovery starts with the outside world, and moves inward as children learn, without necessarily being told what to do. The senses are the link between the outer and inner worlds, and since listening and looking are so important a part of the sensory world, creating an environment where children can learn about the arts of listening and looking, is part of the awakening of intelligence that Krishnamurti spoke about.'

One wonders if Krishnamurti is required reading in the Indian B.Ed curriculum.

Krishnamurthy's views closely echo those of Swami Vivekananda, according to whom, 'The goal of mankind is knowledge ... Now this knowledge is inherent in man. No knowledge comes from outside: it is all inside. What we say a man "knows", should, in strict psychological language, be what he "discovers" or "unveils"; what man "learns" is really what he discovers by taking the cover off his own soul, which is a mine of infinite knowledge.'[3]

Clearly the purpose of education must be to help a pupil learn as a process of discovery. Discovery can scarcely happen without a sense of curiosity. And creating that curiosity in the minds of the students is the purpose of education.

---

[2] R.E. Mark Lee, 'The Arts of Listening, Looking and Learning', *Journal of the Krishnamurti Schools*, Issue No. 4, May 2000.

[3] Swami Vivekananda, Karma-Yoga (1921).

READING AND TEACHING

What if a child is entirely uninterested in a particular subject? Should one merely leave a child not to pursue such a subject? Of course not. As T.S. Eliot says, 'No one can become really educated without having pursued some study in which he took no interest. For it is part of education to interest ourselves in subjects for which we have no aptitude.'

The habit of real reading (and not just mechanical reading and cramming of textbooks) is integral to teaching and education only because reading is the most effective medium for learning about the world.

According to Sir Francis Bacon, 'Read not to contradict and confute; nor to believe and take for granted; nor to find talk and discourse; but to weigh and consider. Some books are to be tasted, others to be swallowed, and some few to be chewed and digested: that is, some books are to be read only in parts, others to be read, but not curiously, and some few to be read wholly, and with diligence and attention.'

In other words, reading provides for continuing education. In this sense, education and continuing education through reading become important whether one is rich or poor, employed or unemployed, royalty or pauper, if one is to lead a dignified, meaningful and a happy life. Of course, if one wishes to pursue the happiness of the ignorant, that's different. Education cannot touch such a person!

True, if children do not see a role model in their parents, if they do not see their parents spending any time ever in a bookshop or library, or buying and reading books at home, or never reading out from a book to them, it is less likely that the kids will learn to make reading a habit. That is a gap that schools which take into account the particular circumstances of the children will have to fill in.

Thus, my short response to the above CEO's concern will be to advise him to change the paradigm of education in the minds of those children and parents. If an educational institution cannot educate children about what education is, it's downhill all the way!

READING AND PROFESSIONALS

It must be said that the habit of reading needs to be inculcated not just among children. The advice perhaps holds equally or more for a large body of adults whose reading habit is either absent or dormant. If you are a mid-career professional – even one of those impatient forever-on-the-run sprinters in life – ask yourself when you last read a full article, leave alone a whole book, relating to your profession. If your conscience prevents you from providing an honest answer, you need to ask yourself the next question: How then do you hope to keep abreast of developments in your profession and get ahead in the 'competition' that you have set out to beat as a sprinter? A smile and a shoeshine may be useful, but hardly enough. You need to read, read and read throughout life.

THE SECOND QUESTION

This question, asked during the course of a talk at the Rotary Club on a theme similar to the one I gave in the school above, went like this: The parents were in the habit of reading. They did buy books for the children. While their kids had responded to their exhortations to do well in school and were more or less among the top two or three in their class, they spent practically all their time at home watching television. The hold of the various music channels and such over the teenage kids was such that they simply didn't want to 'waste' their time reading, except the textbooks that 'had to be read'. To any exhortations to read, their quip was: We are doing fine at school, aren't we? So the question from one of the parents was:

HOW CAN PARENTS INTRODUCE THE READING HABIT AMONG THEIR KIDS FOR THE WIDER DEVELOPMENT OF THEIR MIND?

Now that's the tricky part about going around lecturing. Questions are flung at you that can momentarily render you agape. Now this is hardly a question that one can answer during the tail-end of the question-answer session of a pre-dinner lecture! But that does not render the question invalid either!

Look at it this way. When a child applies to a new school, what is the criterion typically employed? A test or an entrance examination. What is the nature of these tests? Not very different from the regular curriculum-linked tests. But how much weight is given to a child's other attributes, such as curiosity, creativity, and risk-taking ability? Perhaps little. Not because the schools think these are irrelevant, perhaps, but because these attributes are more difficult to measure.

Thus, the answer to this question is the same as the answer to the first question. After all, if, like parents, the schools' view of education is also short-sighted, and implicitly oriented to examination performance, rankings, rote learning, strict obedience, etc., are we surprised if kids consider the objective of education as achieved if they are scoring well in their exams? Naturally, when they grow up, they pass on the same understanding of education to their offspring. That's exactly the reason we need to re-define education.

At the risk of reiteration, a good education ought to inculcate curiosity, confidence, creativity, risk-taking attitude and cooperation in the children. As Einstein says, 'Education is what is left behind after you have forgotten what you learnt in the classroom.'

The fact is that once kids reach their teens without having picked up the habit of reading, it gets increasingly difficult to get them into the habit. The problem in fact becomes twofold. It's not simply a question of getting them to read. You also have to wean them away from whatever else it is that they have gotten into the habit of, before you can get them to read. That is why the relative priorities in life must comprise an adequate mix of knowledge, entertainment, sports, studies, adventure, music, and arts. That is what holistic education is all about. And that kind of approach to life has to start young.

So how do parents inculcate this habit of reading in their children? It may be true that the number of books at home and the reading habits among the children from these homes are highly correlated. So then, will buying a load of books and stacking them at home suffice for the children to take up the reading habit? Not necessarily. Remember, we only said the number of books at home and the reading habits of children are highly correlated. We said nothing about causality. A township that suffers from many diseases may have a large number of doctors. Thus, the number of doctors and the number of people suffering with diseases in the town has a high positive correlation; so could you say then that the presence of many doctors in a town causes more diseases? Wouldn't a paucity of doctors lead to even more uncured diseases, so that paucity of doctors and high incidence of diseases could also be highly positively correlated? So you see, establishing causality can be tricky!

So perhaps buying a whole library of books for the home is not the easy solution to encourage your child's interest in reading. In fact, why children from families that have a lot of books are more given to reading may be working as follows:

What kinds of families tend to have a lot of books at home? Probably, families of educated folks who themselves read. Such folks are more likely to be of scholarly bent than others. Assuming that in the nature versus nurture debate, each plays a 50 per cent role as suggested by most research, it may be that children from such families are in any case more likely to be disposed towards scholarship through inherited genes and hence more likely to take up reading as a habit. Nurture may play a role in that not only do children see the parents reading, but adults in the family read out to the children from a very young age. Environment may play a role to the extent that if books are lying around, a kid is more likely to pick one up at some time or the other, perhaps find it absorbing and then try another. At best it exacerbates the habit of a kid with the right genes and at worst it does nothing for a kid who is not so endowed. Thus, stacking up the house with a lot of books might help, but only halfway. And merely stacking up the home with books, without the family elders genuinely being book lovers, may only be a halfway house – as likely to succeed as not.

By the same token, parents who are not themselves interested in reading may not necessarily succeed in getting their children to read merely by stacking up the home with books. The presence of the books may create an enabling environment, but in the absence of the parental role model, the child may yet not develop a great interest in reading. And yet, it may be worthwhile to remember that an enabling environment still contributes to 50 per cent of what one is or is not.

Answering a question – 'You seem so well read; tell us how it all started?' – at the Berkshire Hathaway Shareholders meeting at Omaha (2008), Warren Buffett replies saying, 'My father was a stockbroker, so we had all these financial books in our library. He introduced me to those classics and I got into them.... The beauty about reading and learning is that the more you learn the more you want to learn.'[4]

Of course from time to time, there may come along a child prodigy for whom the normal rules of parenting, schooling, and reading may not apply! One does off and on come across or read about young prodigies like a Ramanujam, or someone who wins the Wimbledon championship or bats for India Eleven at seventeen, or sets up his own software company at sixteen or floats his own airline at twenty, or gives professional concerts at nine. With or without the right parenting or the right schooling, these kids may yet go on to achieve what he or

---

[4]   From the website of the Bombay Stock Exchange.

she was destined to achieve. But we are obviously not talking of such cases that are few and far between.

OTHER REASONS TO READ

No one can deny that if you want to keep your body fit physically, you need to exercise regularly. In other words, physical fitness must become one's habit and become a routine. If one just ate junk food all the time and did no physical exercise, one would put on weight, grow lazy and probably ill.

Often we do not seem to think that the same principle applies to our mental well-being as well. If we provide the mental faculties no nourishment, give them no opportunity to think, ponder and reflect, and feed the brain nothing but passive feed like television, the brain is bound to degenerate, slowly but surely. It loses the habit of thinking. It loses the habit of learning. It stagnates.

Reading, solving puzzles and problems are activities that make one think actively. They stimulate the brain into thinking and help build images in the mind, stir creativity, build vocabulary, and improve language. All this helps information to sink in, be processed, retained and assimilated to become knowledge. As the knowledge base expands, reading and problem solving becomes increasingly more efficient and the learning curve becomes steeper. And lastly, regular reading sharpens intellectual acumen leading to superior conversation and social skills, and thus to true education.

When one exercises more and more, one's sense of well-being is assuaged only when one continues to exercise. It is the same with reading. Once you are in the habit of reading, your sense of mental well-being is assuaged only when you read more and more. Just as people may exercise in small packages or in long uninterrupted bouts as may suit their physiology, reading may be in spurts or in long stretches to suit one's mental capacity.

Again, just as constant exercising builds one's stamina to enable one to exercise slightly harder, reading leads to one's ability to read more complex material. In fact, it is the more complex reading that stretches one's mental capacity. That is why a good reader often switches between fiction and non-fiction. Besides, the more one reads on a given subject, the faster one tends to read other material on the same or similar subject. One who never reads is a laboured reader just as one who never exercises huffs and puffs when called upon to exercise.

HOBBIES

I know of no surveys or research reports to back my observation, but it seems to me that relatively few adults in our country, as compared to people elsewhere in the world, pursue serious hobbies or interests, or pursue any hobby or interest seriously, aside from their bread-winning vocations. While the reasons for this may be many, the fact does make us somewhat duller as a people. And what is more, it also takes away something from us as well-rounded people. It is difficult to believe that an average adult is uni-dimensional.

Also in our country, our vocations and hobbies or interests do not necessarily coincide, unlike in many of the developed countries. For example, when one views TV channels like the National Geographic, Discovery, Animal Planet, Fox History or Travel and Living, it becomes immediately evident that most of the individuals one sees on the many programmes are evidently enjoying what they do for a living. This is hardly the case in our socio-economic conditions, so that our vocations and interests rarely coincide. In such a situation it is all the more a tragedy that few of us pursue hobbies and interests parallel to our vocations. As a consequence we end up developing into uni-dimensional people, even if we were not so to begin with. Most of us develop or nurture few interests outside our work environment. Our idea of a good holiday is often a good day's nap. Not many of us try our hand at amateur carpentry or cookery or theatre over a weekend. We end up bottling up our potential and fail to discover the full range of possibilities that lurk inside us. We rarely live our lives fully and do not realize that it is never too late to begin!

And unfortunately, what we do to ourselves, we do to our children. Given the excessive pressures of student life today, with practically no free time from school, tuitions and other coaching, and given our impatience towards our child's time 'whiled away on hobbies', fewer and fewer children today seem to develop a deep interest in active hobbies. It would appear that wittingly or unwittingly, hobbies have little place in the world of an Indian school kid, who is forever being made to run a sprint.

These kids will obviously grow into adults with no hobbies and interests either. True, it is difficult to spot in a kid collecting matchbox covers a future art collector; or in a child making cardboard cars a future automobile designer; or a future professional percussionist in a kid spending time in the school band. But even assuming that not every kid with a trivial hobby may grow into a major aficionado of art or artifacts, or with a deep passion for something or the other, shouldn't a child be encouraged in the pursuit of some such trivia for its own sake? After all, much of life's pleasures do come out of everyday trivia and trinkets, right? Probably as parents in India, we do not encourage such pursuits today because a kid spending time to raid a garbage dump collecting matchbox covers, or stroking metal discs at the school band is taking away time from that crucial tuition or coaching camp.

True we may be driving our kid around from the tennis camp to the music lessons to the karate camp. But I wonder if we can truly count these activities among hobbies, particularly if a kid is more or less pushed into these activities by parental or peer pressures. Ideally a hobby is something a child finds to do naturally. It has nothing to do with what is fashionable; or what will be useful in later life; or what is chic in the parent's peer group. A hobby, particularly in childhood, is all about spontaneity. It is the unconscious sprouting of a child's intrinsic interests. It's about an activity that has the highest probability of staying with the child, as the child becomes an adult. It's about a childhood passion that may or may not become an adult's learned pastime or even profession, but would certainly add a dimension to the child's personality as the child becomes a man. A hobby is best picked up when young because then it has the best chance of becoming a way of life.

So then, how can education in schools be more child-oriented? How can parents help?

10 SCHOOLING FOR MEDIOCRITY

> *The founding fathers in their wisdom decided that children were an unnatural strain on parents. So they provided jails called schools, equipped with tortures called education. School is where you go between when your parents can't take you and industry can't take you.*

—JOHN UPDIKE[1]

CONSIDER AN AVERAGE SCHOOL. WHAT ARE THE values that a typical school in our country engenders? How interesting is the curriculum or how interestingly is it taught? Does it arouse the child's curiosity in a subject and make a child eager to learn? Is the kind of competition a child is exposed to in our primary schools, leave alone secondary schools, healthy?

A typical school is long on authority and discipline, and short on spontaneity and freedom – the two main traits that define most kids. A wide body of research studies shows that learning happens best under conditions of spontaneity and

---

[1] William H. Pritchard, *Updike: America's Man of Letters*, University of Massachusetts Press, 2000.

enjoyment rather than under coercion and regimen, and yet most of our schools act as if they were entirely innocent of such knowledge. Most, if not all schools today take pride in institutionalizing after-school tuitions. Increasingly, it is as if the regular schools are there merely to clock the children's time away from home in boring indoor custody, and learning must happen (if we call the rote-based conditioning as *learning*) through tuitions. Most schools are overcrowded. Such is the acute paucity of open spaces in our towns and cities that most schools have consumed much of their open grounds for expansion of buildings over the years, and have practically no playfields to call their own. Under the circumstances, there is little opportunity for the kids to participate in major team sports within the confines of the schools. The average school kid today has a rather dull life, bereft of all opportunities to develop his personality; bereft of all spontaneity emblematic of childhood; devoid of all teamwork from which a kid could learn a lifetime of people skills and dispossessed of any genuine opportunity to learn or to 'learn to learn'.

Says Dr Anita Rampal of Delhi University, commenting on our primary schooling system:

'We all know of multiplication tables that children are heartlessly made to learn "by heart", but at an SSK (Shishu Shiksha Kendra) training we saw the use of addition tables, unflinchingly repeated over and over and over again. "Ek jog ek dui, dui jog ek teen, teen jog ek…" (One plus one two, two plus one three, three plus one four…). In addition, there was an absurd attempt to render it "joyful", with little understanding of how children learn concepts of "number" or addition. All kind of cosmetic padding was added to the exercise (literally so!) which resulted in the 70-plus [septuagenarian] trainer hopping single-legged, perilously unsteady, while chanting the addition tables.'[2]

This mindlessness graduates into mindless rote learning, in the form of tuitions and *kunjis* (help books) and 'professional' coaching centres in higher classes, stuffing millions of young minds with zillion bits of information and yet leaving them completely uneducated. William Butler Yeats said, 'Education is not the filling of a bucket, but rather the lighting of a fire.' However, by giving our children answers to memorize, when they should be given problems to solve, not only are our schools mostly busy filling a bucket, they are doing so only to douse the fire, if any.

And it is this system that we not only perpetuate, but also greatly reinforce, by further exhorting our children to sprint. We compound the felony, as it were, by asking our children to run a mindless, purposeless sprint. The end result is that most of our students graduating from our educational system – whether primary, secondary or tertiary – are not only conditioned on rote-learning, but sub-standard for the respective level of education.

As parents, we may not be able to wave a magic wand and change how our schools are run or how or what they teach, but surely it is entirely for us to decide whether we counteract the system as required and try to change its bad parts or reinforce the good ones?

---

[2] Anita Rampal, *Unpacking the 'quality' of schools*, ARE WE LEARNING? – A symposium on ensuring quality elementary education, No. 536 (April 2004).

WHAT CAN PARENTS DO?

If real learning does not happen in our schools, how will making our children sprint in a mad race help? As enlightened parents, can't we create an atmosphere, at least at home, where they do not feel pressured to run this mindless race? How do we do this?

By encouraging our children to read. By inculcating in them the desire to know, to learn, and to find out. By instilling in them a love for learning – what they want to learn, when they want to learn, and at a pace that suits them best, with a gentle nudge here and a look there from the parents. By identifying the children's strengths – whether in games, sports, arts, crafts, or anything else that develops their skills and personality meaningfully – and pushing them gently in the direction of those strengths rather than pushing them at a pace and in a direction that goes completely counter to what the child enjoys or identifies with.

As long as a child shows adequate interest in the process of learning, it may be best to let him read what interests him most. For example, if a child deeply interested in cricket takes to reading about the nuances of cricket, the child has already learnt to associate reading with learning. As the child grows and gets interested in other things, he would certainly read up on those things. That is the essence of education.

Adults will do well to remember that a child will want to read what is enjoyable to him at that age; not what the adult thinks is best. Unless a child takes to reading something truly unhealthy, allowing sufficient autonomy in reading will inculcate a genuine interest in the habit.

True, a child may not always know where he wants to go or what his strengths are. Why children, most of us – even into our middle age – often do not know exactly what is it that we are chasing in life. Money? Fame? Travel? Family bonding? Happiness? Why expect a kid to know then? The fact is that neither our schools, nor we as parents, allow a child any time to discover himself. And we imagine that pushing a child in a random direction or a direction of our choice is preferable to letting or helping the child discover the natural direction of his calling. We forget that 'learning is something children do, NOT something done to children', to use the words of Alfie Kohn, an American educationist.

UNDERSTAND THE FEAR OF EVALUATION

I came across this parent who was rather concerned that his child was pathologically scared of exams. Parents usually believe that their children are scared of exams because they are not suitably prepared. In truth, examination blues are a common phenomenon. Some children are more scared of examinations than others. The fear of examination may not always be about being underprepared. Let us face it. Examinations are all about evaluating an individual. Even adults do not really like being evaluated, as most of us find during annual performance measurement time in our own organizations! I am sure our cricketers do not like to be evaluated based on each outing on each innings. Academics are often cagey about being evaluated on their citation index or the number of their publications year after year. No Bollywood actor likes to be evaluated on the basis of each film. I am sure Sania Mirza will be mortified if she were to be evaluated on the basis of each of her outings onto a tennis court. So then, why should a kid love his exams any more?

WHAT DO EXAMS AND ENTRANCE TESTS EVALUATE?

As for routine school examinations, more often than not, they evaluate a child's capacity to learn by rote and reproduce, on a given day, segments from their textbooks. In most schools the evaluation process allows very little degree of freedom to a child's individuality and analytical capacity. The evaluation methodology is geared towards making the system simple for the teachers rather than assessing the true abilities and achievements of a child as measured in terms of analytical power and genuine learning. That is why most schools operate on the 'there is only one correct answer to a question' principle. Given this fact, it would appear so unfair to judge a child as a 'failure' based on such examinations.

What about the entrance tests for national institutions? Clearly, when a hundred individuals compete, nay scramble, for a single seat based on fuzzily defined characteristics of intelligence, knowledge, personality and such, there can be no testing procedure that can ensure that the one out of the hundred who made it was the 'best candidate'.

There are several reasons for this. Firstly, all selection procedures have two kinds of statistical errors, namely, Type 1 error and Type 2 error. The first pertains to the possibility that a deserving candidate does not make it through the selection procedure. The second pertains to the possibility that an undeserving student makes it. A good selection procedure has relatively low incidence of both kinds of errors, while poor procedures have a high incidence. The cost of bringing down these errors to zero is enormous and it is practically impossible, even without factoring in the challenges of defining 'a best candidate'. Over the years, thanks to the coaching classes repeatedly conditioning tens of thousands of students into test-cracking machines, the discriminating ability of the entrance tests has been falling steadily, increasing the incidence of Type 1 and Type 2 errors in the process. In addition, often the difference between those who 'make it' and those who don't, with regard to their qualifying cut-off scores, could be razor-thin. At the cut-off points, often there is an enormous crowding, so that a single mark less could mean five hundred candidates above you. Thus, at the margin, the difference between whether or not one makes it into these competitive tests could be the side of the bed one got off.

Under these conditions, how serious a judgment is it on your child's intelligence or knowledge, if he 'fails' to make it through one of these national tests? Given that life is a long-distance run, can that one test determine the 'worth' of the child?

WHAT WOULD YOU SAY ABOUT THIS KID?

Let me narrate something about a teenage daughter of a friend of mine. The youngster is a pleasant and social teenager. She is an average student by most conventional parameters – she may or may not crack any of the national-level entrance tests post her school finals. But here is what happened once, though the sequence of events was discovered much later and not as it was unfolding.

The 16-year-old had noticed that in her apartment block, the drivers, watchmen and domestic staff did not have a toilet. Finding this an unacceptable situation, she contacted the building secretary for a solution. As expected, she was given several reasons why a toilet could not be constructed. A little bit of probing and inspection convinced her that these reasons were probably genuine. Most would have reconciled to the status quo at this stage. Not this young lady. She went into Google search and found an Indian company that was making reasonably priced portable toilets, which could be attached to the sewerage system and water pipes. Armed with requisite information on the deal, she went back to the building secretary again and at the time of writing this chapter, she was in the process of having the secretary place an order.

For a few days her mother had been wondering why the girl was rushing in and out of home at odd times, when to her delight the matter came to her notice. The youngster was doing what she was doing entirely on her own initiative, not to impress anyone, not as a school project, and certainly not as a do-gooding initiative. She saw a wrong and was working to right it. She wasn't taking a minor obstacle as a final answer. She was willing to push herself to find answers. Who cares if she is 'average' in her school exams? She is outstanding in the school of life and is bound to make a very significant citizen some day.

DO WE PREPARE OUR KIDS TO FACE FAILURE?

There is something else that neither schools nor parents prepare a child for – failure – even though failure is as much a part of life's portfolio as success is. It may well be that a child's self-esteem develops with early successes. And yet, can self-esteem be really developed without also teaching a child to cope with real or perceived failures?

People with the best of abilities encounter failure in life at one stage or the other. The best of authors face dozens of rejections before tasting success. The best of inventors and researchers face hordes of failures before hitting upon the right solutions. The best of sportspeople lose matches. The best of generals lose battles. And yet, a child flunking a test, exam or a year is regarded as the worst shame! The kid is often labelled and treated as dull, negligent, non-studious or even good for nothing or a no-hoper, again and again, directly or indirectly! Teachers think nothing of shaming such children in front of the class. Parents think nothing of running them down before others or reminding them of the failure at every opportunity. On occasion, these pressures from parents, teachers and even peers can be such that in the extreme, a child would rather face death than failure.

Carol Dweck, in her book *Mindset*, makes some interesting observations on the reaction of some children to failure to solve puzzles given to them.[3] Ordinarily, one expects a child who fails to solve a puzzle to experience a sense of failure. The author refers to this kid who when he failed to solve the puzzle, rather than feeling disheartened, 'rubbed his hands together, smacked his lips, and cried out, 'I love a challenge!' Yet another kid, labouring hard at the problem, looked up happily, and said with authority, 'You know, I was *hoping* this would be

---

[3]   Carol S. Dweck, *Mindset*, Ballantine Books (2007).

informative!' Clearly, how one deals with failure is a question of mindset that will determine how the child will fulfil his potential in the future. Should not schools and parents alike help more and more kids to develop a more positive attitude towards failures?

But how often do we teach our children to really learn from and cope with failure? How often do our children succeed in turning a failure into a positive mindset? The interesting thing, as Dweck points out, is that these children didn't even know they were failing! They thought they were learning! It is precisely this spirit that we may be extinguishing with our constant pressure on children to perform.

According to Randy Pausch, the author of *The Last Lecture*, '...a lot of parents don't realize the power of their words. Depending on a child's age and sense of self, an offhand comment from Mom or Dad can feel like a shove from a bulldozer.'[4]

So next time your child fails at something, you may want to think how you want your child to react to that failure before you say something.

FROM TEACHING TO LEARNING

Most of our schools are ineffective because they usually attempt to teach, while they should be helping children to learn. What is the difference between a teaching-oriented educational system vis-à-vis a learning-oriented system? A

---

[4] Randy Pausch and Jeffrey Zaslow, *The Last Lecture*, Hyperion (2008).

teaching-oriented system by definition looks upon teaching as a duty to be performed – the duty being to *teach*. The emphasis is obviously not on whether the student *learns* but on whether the teacher *teaches*. Well, examinations and tests are supposed to measure whether students learn, one might say. But in reality, isn't our entire examination system geared towards giving children answers to remember, rather than problems to solve? Would this not encourage short-term memory that produces good examination results at the cost of encouraging in children a spirit of enquiry and making them curious scholastically? Isn't the emphasis then on regurgitation of answers rather than on building capacity to learn?

Excessive emphasis on teaching-orientation has the danger that even in such schools where teachers do appear in the classrooms, teaching can be easily reduced to a ritual. In fact, let us contrast the government schools with the private ones. In a majority of our government schools little teaching (or learning) actually happens. In the private schools – at least the better ones – where some teaching does happen, the grind typically involves not merely lecturing some six hours a day, but also assigning homework, checking dozens upon dozens of exercise books, conducting weekly tests and correcting those answer papers, preparing progress cards, tracking weak students, meeting parents, disciplining children and generally putting up with the colossal din that the little rascals can make!

Where are the vocational skills in the curriculum? Where is the play-oriented learning? Where is the learning by doing (except in a small minority of schools)? Where are the group-assignments? How frequent are the field trips? Where are self-learning opportunities? A sense of discovery?

In short, where is the time for children to learn? With a single teacher burdened with all these tasks, it would be a miracle if the teaching can actually result in much learning, beyond some conditioned regurgitation of answers.

In contrast to a teaching-oriented educational system, a learning-oriented system concentrates on helping the students to learn. In fact it even does better than *helping students to learn*. A good learning system and a good teacher help students *learn to learn*. Such a system changes the nature of a teacher's engagement from teaching to enabling. In other words, in a learning-oriented system, facilitators, rather than conventional teachers, are what are needed. Tools such as learning systems, workbooks, encyclopedias, educational software, educational games, labs, experiments, exploration, research, projects and group activities take precedence. Classroom teaching with the teacher on one end and the students on the other is minimal.

But creating such a system, though superior to the teaching-oriented system, calls for a great resolve. It calls for enlightened intellectuals and not lazy civil servants to create such a system. Such a system requires, not merely a conceptual ability, but a strong and ongoing will and resolve to implement, which our school administrations, civil servants and politicians alike, lack. It calls for ongoing innovation and experimentation. It needs us to change systems within educational institutions – from curriculum development to evaluation. And it calls for a lot more. This is perhaps the reason why we have assiduously stuck to our truly mediocre educational system, which seems particularly designed to extinguish any spark of originality that a child may show.

HE WHO LEARNT FROM FAILURES

As we have been talking about competitors, here is the story of a competitor, who all his life has competed only with himself, and who probably learnt much more from life than from school.

Born in 1950, he is from a little known village called Rajam in Srikakulum district of Andhra Pradesh. His parents, married in their teens, had a small gold and trading business in the village that entitled them to the status of 'an average middle class family'. The boy's grandfather had passed away when his father was still young. The boy himself was the third among seven siblings – four brothers and three sisters. Clearly the boy had far from a grand starting point.

Early schooling was in a government school – a local Telugu-medium institution. The boy was a fairly bright and active fellow, albeit somewhat naughty. Languages were his nemesis. He excelled in neither Telugu nor English. The parents themselves were rather indifferent to his academic prowess, as parents in that era with several children to raise were wont to be. No one particularly cared if the young fellow actually went to school every single day or played truant now and then. And the boy seems to have had few qualms taking advantage of this lax supervision to feed his adventurous thirst. As the family owned a small shed outside the village for business purposes, the young schoolboy would often escape from the large family to that private little space and return home next morning, with no one the wiser! Nor was he beyond pedalling 50 to 60 km to catch a movie, again with no one in the family any the wiser. The freewheeling spirit of the boy was certainly adventurous, even if it appears somewhat thin on discipline.

And expectedly, the boy failed his SSLC (Secondary School Leaving Certificate, equivalent to Class X or high school final) examination, as did his friends! The father made his peremptory declaration, 'No further studies! Come and join the family business.'

For the boy, destined to change the infrastructural face of the country one day, this was the electric shock that would change his track. At this crucial juncture in his life came a remarkable teacher, Damiri Venkata Rao, *Doramastru* (Teacher Sir). The lad realized, thanks to this one noteworthy teacher (still active today), that even though he had flunked his SSLC, he still wanted to and could study further. The dim realization that without a basic grounding in academics, he would at best have a mediocre future was an intuitive one. The boy coaxed his family doctor to counsel his father to cough up the requisite fees for repeating his SSLC, to little avail. The father stood steadfast. In his view, as both his elder sons, and now the third one, had failed the SSLC, it was evident that it was no joke to pass SSLC. In any case, ultimately he had to come back and join the family business. So why waste time and money now? Nor were his mother and brothers in favour of his repeating his SSLC. But then, destiny's children are not easily thwarted.

The boy prevailed upon his father to support his SSLC once again. The boy realized that one of his major weaknesses was English. His grammar and sentence formation skills were abysmal. The boy had realized that even though he had come out really badly in English, it was not on account of poor

teaching, but because of his own shortcomings. He went back
to one of his other teachers, Patnayak Mastru, who had taught
him language in class VII and VIII. With a strong resolution
to work specifically on his weaknesses, the lad put his nose
to the grindstone and worked on elementary grammar and
fundamentals. He also learnt his early values from this very
teacher.

There is no awakening like self-awakening. You cannot
beat motivation into a teenager. Nor is failure or the shock
of it always a bad thing for a teenager. Jolted by his failure,
dissuaded by his parents, the self-motivated boy worked hard.
So hard in fact that he ended the year by topping not merely his
school but the whole mandal under which his village, Rajam,
came. He had scored 422 out of 500 – a healthy 84.4 per cent
marks – a wonderment in an era when scoring a first class (60
per cent) was considered a scholastic achievement.

The case for his family to dissuade him from pursuing
his pre-university course (PUC) was now weak. Rejected by
Loyola College, Vijaywada because he had passed his SSLC
in the second attempt, the boy settled for a college in Bobbli,
the adjoining village. Chastened now by his earlier failure and
the attitude of his parents to his continuing his education,
the boy continued to work hard and once again topped the
college PUC with distinction. This, aided further by the fact
that he obtained twelfth rank in the provisional selection for
BE, enabled him to join the Engineering College in Andhra
University, Vizag. By now, the parents, pleasantly surprised
by the boy's more-than-decent showing in academics, were
beginning to veer around to allowing him to go his way.

The boy moved into the university hostel. He continued to
do well in academics. He would help his friends in whatever

way possible. His popularity drove him to contest elections, win and become the secretary of the College of Engineering Students Union. He saw in this role not an empty seat of power but an opportunity to improve the hostel conditions and to serve the student community in a myriad other ways. He also became active in extracurricular activities such as college functions and the college magazine. He was also married while still a student of engineering, as was the rural norm of the time.

Through all this, one characteristic remained: a large circle of friends. If he was going to be a leader of men, this is where he learnt the ropes. He was a people's person. The single-most important quality of the youngster was the ability to carry his friends along. He was already mastering the art of 'making friends and influencing people'. Well, he finally passed his mechanical engineering with merit and was now out in the wide open world.

The boy, a young man now, returned to his village to take stock of his life. The father, disillusioned at the way the business was going, had divided the family assets of two trucks and Rs. 12 lakh into five parts – four for the four brothers and one for the mother. So the dilemma before him was whether to start a small industry of his own with his share of funds, or take up employment as an educated professional or join the family business. His heart was set on entrepreneurship.

About this time, there was an agency for AP Scooters on offer in Vizag. The young engineer was quite sold on the idea and tried every trick in the bag to bag the agency. He failed – his first failure as an adult. Next he joined the family in buying out an oil mill, but the project ran aground due to some sales tax problems. So the oil mill was leased out and so were the trucks. His second failure. So willy-nilly he turned to the possibility of employment. He was interviewed by a ferro-alloy company near Rajam for a job which would bring a monthly salary of Rs. 500. He was rejected, thanks to his student political career, which for some reason gave him the aura of a communist! The third failure of the adult!

By now, somewhat confused and indecisive, the young man opted for the haven of an M.Tech, even as he continued trying to set up an industry of his own. But six months into his M.Tech, he got an offer of employment in AP Paper Mills at Rs. 400 per month, and quit the course. He did well enough to gain an increment. The youngster trained hard in the workshop at night shifts. However, his restless heart seemed to scream that this was not for him. Even though he was offered an increased salary of Rs. 1,000 per month, he quit AP Paper Mills to join the Public Works Department. But then destiny's children aren't known to be held by the PWD for long! He quit it after two months to work in some trading business with his brothers.

At this time, the demise of a brother-in-law brought additional economic stringencies upon the family. His widowed sister and her five young children were now part of the young man's responsibility, he being the only truly educated man in the family.

By now, perennially and vigorously in search of an opportunity to set up an industry of his own, he had a strong intuition about the sugar industry and wished to start a sugar mill. He plunged headlong, but quietly, like a seasoned diver, to work towards his silent objective of obtaining a licence.

He and two elder brothers would often stay in Chennai during the off-season for collections of their receivables. During this period, the young man managed to find a window of opportunity to pay an advance for purchase of a sick sugar mill, without the knowledge of his brothers – much to their nervousness, of course! Against overwhelming odds, from having to renegotiate the deal with the seller, to getting a letter of recommendation from the state industries department, to obtaining the approval for transfer of licence from the sugar commissioner in Kolkata, he worked his way through tenaciously. From dismantling the sick unit from the Ambattur industrial estate to relocating it in Rajam, he left nothing to chance. All this had been achieved in the face of tough competition from other companies. This was the youth's first smell of success in entrepreneurship.

Well, let us take a pause and consolidate our findings of the early life of our youngster. It is certainly not a spectacular start in life. The boy came from a rural setting in a district that even today counts among the most educationally backward in the country. His was an academically indifferent family. He went to an unknown school. He experienced little discipline or control at home, which appears to contribute to his early, if not delinquency, certainly somewhat wayward ways. He flunked his SSLC. He had parents who were least keen that he study further. He had no clarity on what he wanted to do.

And what do we find on the flip side? A fundamentally nice and responsible youngster. One who is extremely bright, notwithstanding what his early school records say. One with a strong sense of adventure. One who is not easily fazed by failure. In fact, one who is made by his failures. One who is nothing if not a people's man. One who can put in sustained hard work. One who is tenacious like a bull dog. One who has an independent mind and yet strong family affiliation. One who is never wanting in efforts. One who is human enough to be confused but resolute enough not to lose his final focus. One who is not infallible, but is quick to get up and move on. Fortunately for him, his parents did not succeed in pushing him into something that he did not want to do, namely the family business.

So what do we have in balance? A young Malli Babu, aka G.M. Rao, aka GMR. Yes, Grandhi Mallikarjuna Rao – the man who spawned a world-class and world-sized empire in half a lifetime, the infrastructure major GMR Group. GMR would never look back after winning that sugar licence. That first licence was his licence to entrepreneurship. With that licence, he had taken the first step in his 1,000-mile march. In time, GMR would get into banking, insurance, power, roads, airports and real estate and catapult his group in a mere twenty years into the big daddies club of business. It needs to be said that many of his boyhood friends are working with him even today, and often in key positions.

So exactly what lessons do we find in G.M. Rao's early life that fit our thesis? As most successful entrepreneurs are, GMR comes out as a people's man. The one remarkable fact about him is he rarely forgets a face or a name. Friends to him are for life. You cannot see GMR without a permanently happy and childlike smile. Hard work for him is an act of faith. As a student when repeating his SSLC, he did not work hard to top the school or his Mandal; he never competed with others; he worked hard to make up for the learning he had not achieved;

to do well against his own benchmark and not to score more than anybody else.

GMR is still a learner. It is not unusual for him to stop any of his senior executives mid-sentence to understand exactly what a particular expression or phrase means! He is a man of detail. Just as he was while he was working to clear his SSLC the second time or when he won his sugar licence. Even today, while presiding over a personal wealth of a billion dollars plus, he works eighteen hours a day; seven days a week. Obviously money does not motivate him. Had that been the case he should have had every motivation to slow down once he had made big bucks. But it is his steady trot of progress, his working against his own benchmarks, forever excelling that little bit, forever growing that bit extra, forever learning and forever having faith that makes GMR a true *karmayogi*.

It may well be that the early symptoms of the great entrepreneur-to-be were hidden in his adventurous spirit. Could it be that the laissez-faire attitude of his parents taught him to make decisions for himself? There can be no doubt that his early friends were his profitable investments in human resource. If he wanted to see a movie, a 120 km bicycle ride to and fro was of no concern. If he wanted to build an airport, spending Rs. 30 crore just to be able to make a successful bid was no issue. He never competed against others – not when in school, not when in business. He sets his own targets and goes after them. He was a learner then. He is a learner now. He was focused then. He is focused now. Had he, as a child, been broken in with sprinting skills, taught, tutored or badgered into academic grades, coached into a school team and made to take failure as the end of the world, he would probably have grown into yet another engineer working 10 to 5 for a living.

It may indeed be argued that the kind of parental indifference that GMR faced could well have been counter-productive. The independence to skip school and run off to movies may not be the best way to rear one's children. Nor is it our case that children need to be given that extreme degree of independence. The point being made is that excessive control does not necessarily shape the character of a child better. The best thing to do may be to let the kid grow at his own pace (which is not the same as under-parenting), rather than kill the spontaneity of the child with over-parenting or with stress on overachievement.

GMR came from a backward area. He belonged to a community that boasted of no power – not economic, not political, not social, and not feudal. He had no start whatever to speak of. He was brought up in an India where making money was a dirty word. In the then-India of licence raj, only the already established industrial houses had the licence to industrial captaincy.

Today, though he is one of the most successful entrepreneurs in the country, GMR never competes against others. Even when he bids for a project, he is self-focused and not focused on what the others may bid. 'Am I doing the right thing? Am I doing better than before? Can I improve what I am doing?' These are the questions that drive him.

So how do we want a child to be?

11 IF YOU COULD MAIL-ORDER YOUR CHILD

You don't really understand human nature unless you know why a child on a merry-go-round will wave at his parents every time around — and why his parents will always wave back.

—WILLIAM D. TAMMEUS

LET US GO BACK TO OUR HYPOTHETICAL OPENING QUESTION in chapter 5. The question was: Supposing you could mail-order a child for yourself, which of the two would you want him to be? A thinking and questioning kid, who is not examination-oriented, or one who would read up without questioning and reproduce the 'correct' answers during exams and thus top the class?

Most thinking individuals when specifically asked are bound to see immediately that in the long run, the thinking and questioning kid is bound to be the winner, even though the kid with a good retentive memory seems to do well in examinations here and now. And yet, deep down, they would rather have a thinking and questioning kid who is also examination oriented! The problem is, the two traits do not always coincide.

I recall an incident which would have been outrageously funny, were it not for the sad fact that the true incident was actually brought to my attention by a Professor of Organization Behaviour in a leading business school, who in his fifties was studying for a law degree just to learn law. The incident occurred in a state where, following Hindu-Muslim riots, a hot topic in the first-year law curriculum that year was whether or not the country should have a uniform civil code. Now in this particular university, not unlike universities elsewhere in the country, most exam questions as well as the model answers were from a certain 'Guide' (which is supposedly a 'simplified' substitute for a textbook). Now in an internal examination, this student faced a question on the Uniform Civil Code. He was penalized as his answer did not correspond to the answer provided against the question in the said guide. And what do you think were the kind of answers provided in the Guide on the question of a Uniform Civil Code? The gem that stands out in my memory to this date went something like this:

'Under the Muslim Law in India, a Muslim can divorce his wife by saying Talaq…Talaq…Talaq, while a Hindu cannot divorce his wife that easily, so that he is stuck with his wife even if she is disobedient and ill tempered'! (exclamation mine).

Unbelievable? Believe it!

(Incidentally, this academic, a PhD from a good US university and a scholar of repute, graduated with a second class in his law degree!)

Well, would you really like your child to score a first class in the examination by regurgitating that hilarious answer from the guide?

The entire education system in our country rewards regurgitation more than it rewards reasoning. It rewards memory more than analysis, conformity more than innovation, and mediocrity more than acumen. And that's all the more reason why we will need to counter such a shoddy and pointless system with our own long-term orientation for our children.

PARENTING STYLE

This brings us to the issue of parenting style. We are not really concerned overly with whether the parenting style should be indulgent, authoritarian, authoritative or uninvolved. Our concern here is whether the parenting style is farsighted or short-sighted; whether it is akin to that of a marathon coach or a sprint coach. Pushing, flogging and pressurizing your kids to outperform other kids, in every test, every exam, in every field, year after year after year, is neither desirable nor sustainable and most over-parenting parents are guilty of this. True, it might appear sustainable to us in the short run, as we see the kid surging ahead of the others, but we do not see the cost the child pays in the process. Nor are we able to see how the same kid handled somewhat differently might have turned out.

But how do we know the kid handled differently, in accordance with the long-term approach, would have turned out any better? We don't. But as reasonably intelligent people, we can conjecture. However, we do not have to conjecture hard to realize that running a long distance with a slower and steadier pace probably holds greater promise and enjoyment in life than running it at a breakneck pace throughout.

For example, there could be a youngster who did not do terribly well in his Class XII or did not get into a professional course. But if one is basically smart, well rounded, and with excellent people and communication skills good enough to start with a call centre job or in some marketing outfit, one might well enjoy that job and excel in it, or one could pick up a degree in architecture, or designing or hospitality services or whatever his calling, later in life, after some initial work experience. In fact, such youngsters are often known to do much better than the 'straight from school' types, whose emotional maturity is often less well developed than those who come up at their own pace. This is exactly what happens in the US. Youngsters go for their Masters degrees well past their mid-twenties and in the process, their assimilation of knowledge and the application of knowledge typically end up being much better than their Indian counterparts, who acquire their degrees much earlier.

Most of us watch highly researched features on the National Geographic, Discovery, Animal Planet or History Channel. In most of these channels, one sees youngsters of various backgrounds doing outstanding quality of work, in such diverse fields as photography, wildlife, travel or automobile engineering. Clearly, it would be impossible to say which of these youngsters has a more exciting career. In other words, the career choices of these youngsters appear to be far more diverse than what our own youth seem to opt for.

Working a couple of years after one's graduation, particularly today when career options are opening up like never before, may be well worth the time for youngsters. Often this period of two or three years of work experience before higher education is considered a delay in the start of one's 'real career'. The fact is that this 'delay' of two or three well-spent years is very much a part of one's career, which may well provide an added impetus to one's later career.

As we observed earlier, more often than not, scoring high marks in school is a function of rote memory more than understanding of concepts. How often as parents do we find teachers penalizing students because their responses did not quite tally with the one specifically prescribed by the teacher! And then the children are doubly penalized when as parents we come down hard on them for not having scored sufficiently well in the examinations.

AN EXAMPLE

In this respect, I recall an old incident involving a friend's son, Sahil, when he was five and in Class I. This kid was a thinking kid. Apparently, earlier during the lessons, the class teacher had supplied a list of five wild animals. Forgetting one of the animals listed by the teacher, this kid included 'hare' in lieu of the forgotten option. The teacher marked the choice of hare as wrong and did not award the 'smiley' face. The child questioned the teacher as to why a hare was not a wild animal. The teacher argued that as a hare could also be a pet, it may not always be wild. The kid argued that usually it was a rabbit that was a pet and that a hare was a pet only by exception, just as a cheetah or a deer (the two animals listed in the original five wild animals by the teacher) could also be pets occasionally! Brilliant arguments from a five-year-old, you might think. But the argument did not cut ice with the teacher and the kid has grown up believing (fortunately for him) not only that teachers aren't always right, but that they can be pig-headed as well. I recall that the kid was more upset about his logic not being accepted than not getting that 'smiley'.

YET ANOTHER EXAMPLE

Here is another old story of a friend's eight-year-old son, Harsh. The little boy faced the following question in an examination: 'What does the poet want to convey through his poem titled such and such in the English textbook?' The little fellow simply wrote out the entire poem for an answer.

Sure enough, when the examination papers were given back, he found a cross across his 'answer'. He went home and complained to his mother that the teacher had unfairly crossed out his answer. When the mother saw the answer paper, she too wondered why he had written out the entire poem. When questioned, the boy's logic was simple: The question had not sought his opinion on what the author had wanted to convey in the poem; it had simply asked what the poet had wanted to convey in the poem. According to the boy, the poet had said what he wanted in the words of the poem. So how could his answer be deemed wrong?

The mother – an academic – was impressed by this logic and accompanied him to meet his teacher and explained the boy's stand. She argued that the boy had written the answer with deliberate thinking and well-argued logic and must be rewarded for that. Of course, the teacher laughed in her face and did not consider it necessary to re-visit her stand.

Incidentally both these kids today are doing outstandingly well in life. Perhaps Einstein was dead right when he said, 'It is in fact nothing short of a miracle that the modern methods of instruction have not yet entirely strangled the holy curiosity of inquiry; for this delicate little plant, aside from stimulation, stands mainly in need of freedom…'

So then what is the best time for a child to commence schooling?

12 School them young?

You send your child to the schoolmaster, but 'tis the schoolboys who educate him.

—Ralph Waldo Emerson

OFTEN THE PRESS AND MEDIA EULOGIZE THE YOUNGEST graduate, or youngest grandmaster, or the youngest test cricketer, or even the youngest president. This has probably created an impression that being the youngest in whatever one does is not only desirable but something to be proud of. It is not uncommon for some parents to get their children into schools at the youngest possible age. Being the youngest is also treated as a means of getting a head start in life. It is seen to expand one's career span and for some reason that is considered highly desirable.

True, the genius of child prodigies may often manifest very early in life. A Mozart may well have started playing the keyboard at three and composing music at five. A Pascal might have written a treatise on vibrating bodies by nine. A Von Neumann might have told jokes in classical Greek at six. A Shirley Temple might have won a special Academy Award at seven. At eight, Tiger Woods might have played in the 9-

10 age group, there being no groups for eight-year-olds. But then, what must be remembered is that it was because they were child prodigies (and put in enormous hard work) that they were able to attain such feats. The reverse is not necessarily true. That is, by somehow doing things early, one does not become a child prodigy.

Let me give you a very personal example. I matriculated at thirteen and graduated at seventeen – from SD High School and SD College, Ambala – both affiliated to Panjab University, Chandigarh. And I never received a double promotion in school ever. Those days the educational system did not universally prescribe a minimum age. For whatever reasons, I went to school at two and hung on (not without some help from obliging teachers, who found the idea of someone so young in the class 'cute'). I always refused the subsequent advice from my parents to drop a year. Most contemporaries in my class at the time would have been at least two to three years older. So let me tell you what the consequences of this 'head start' to me were, as I look back.

Let me recount the disadvantages first, of which there have been many. As I was the youngest in the class by two years, virtually every other kid was much bigger and hence better than me in practically all physical sports. Since I considered it infra dig to run against or play with children junior to me in class, I did not win a prize even in a sack race at a class picnic! I was out of all sports and thus never made even a minimal grade in any. The effect to my self-esteem and self-confidence on this count was undoubtedly negative.

The fact that I might at best have been above average, but not a child prodigy by a far shot, took its toll on my academic performance, which throughout my schooling remained far from impressive. I do not recall a single year in school when I might have been among the top three in the class. Thus, I never went up the stage to collect an award either in sports or in academics. What is worse, I was simply not mature enough to come to grips with the concepts that my classfellows seemed to manage with fair ease. I recall having to resort to rote very often to score reasonably well in examinations and tests. I recall my fundamentals being very weak even after I entered college. Once the foundations of subjects like mathematics, physics or chemistry are shaky, it can take a lifetime to correct the problem.

My school social life was no better. I was a target for most school bullies. Having to cope with them made me by nature very aggressive. Thanks to relatively older friends, at twelve I had the knowledge of a fourteen- or fifteen-year-old schoolboy, though not necessarily possessing the sense that went with the older age. Thus, in some ways, I grew up much before I ideally should have. I could never interact with my classmates without wondering whether or not they were a 'bad influence' on me! Most girls in college were older as well, so that I never made a serious boyfriend to the girls I might have cherished! Even after my Masters, I had difficulty landing a good job, because at 19 or 20, I still looked wet behind my ears!

If you are wondering how I survived being the youngest in class over a long academic life, well, the answer, at least to me, is very clear. Though outstanding at nothing, I was above average in more things than most. I learnt to survive the big bully boys with a combination of aggression and a sense of humour. I also learnt the art of making friends fast. I worked hard at and excelled in non-sports activities, such as debating, drawing and chess, making a small mark for myself. And yet, I have always regretted not having followed my parents' advice to drop a year or two.

Of course, I was lucky that my coping strategies broadly worked. But it is easy to see that unless a child is a genius, an early start is more a liability than an asset. Thus, on balance, I would imagine that a kid at the older end of the age range in school is in fact at a distinct advantage.

HOW YOUNG IS TOO YOUNG TO BEGIN SCHOOL?

Well my views were largely anecdotal. Besides, apart from the relative age of a child, there is also an element of the optimal absolute age for a child to enter school. What do serious researchers have to say on the issue?

Malcolm Gladwell in *Outliers* brings out from numerous examples that when children are very young, even an age difference of six months can be significant.[1] When a child is a little bigger or older and hence plays better or answers questions well or with greater confidence, coaches and teachers begin to single out such children for greater attention. Such kids are often held up as examples, showered with extra attention and as they do well, their confidence is further reinforced. Thus, soon the older children tend to outstrip their

---

[1] Malcolm Gladwell, *Outliers: The Story of Success*, Hachette Books, New York, 2008.

younger counterparts in sports as well as academics. Gladwell proves his case with the data that an overwhelming number of baseball or football players in the junior league, and hence in more senior leagues going right up to the national level, tend to be born in January, February and March and very very few in October, November and December. Gladwell finds that this strange phenomenon is owing to the fact that the cut-off age for these leagues typically turns out to be January 1.

Since a child born in the first quarter would be 9 to 12 months older than a child born in the last quarter of the year, there can be a substantial difference between the physical attributes of children born around the extremes of the year. Children born earlier have a head start over children born later. As these older kids do better than their younger counterparts, they are then singled out for special attention by the coaches and they go on to train that much extra. As a consequence, kids born in January, February and March are far more likely to be in the final teams at each level than kids born much later. The same process repeats for the next age group, so that kids born towards the end of the year stand little chance of making it to the teams! It is as if the month in which a child is born is the best predictor of whether or not he will make it to the league teams! Gladwell believes that the same phenomenon holds true in academia as well.

Therefore, schools are better advised to separate their sections, where they have more than one section, based on the age of the children. For example, if children have a cut-off date of July 1 for academic curriculum, one section may comprise children born between July and December and another of children born between January and June. This is sage advice.

Incidentally, the youngest president or the youngest grandmaster or the youngest test cricketer weren't necessarily the youngest in their class in school! For instance, John F. Kennedy, the youngest US president ever at 43, was 23 when he got his Bachelor of Science degree from Harvard College in 1940.

According to TimesOnline of UK (7 April 2009), 'Starting school at the age of four is too young for children and rarely helps them get ahead, most teachers think.' The survey of the Association of Teachers and Lecturers, involving some 740 school staff, found 'widespread support for a later starting age. Almost a third of teachers believe children should be at least six years old before they start school.'

According to yet another study quoted in TimesOnline UK (6 September 2007), '...children in France, Portugal, Belgium, and Norway start school at 6, while the school starting age in many Scandinavian countries is 7. This is the starting age in Finland, where students recently beat those from 39 other countries to come out tops in maths, science and reading, according to a study by the Programme for International Student Assessment.'

Well, we get the drift. There seems to be ample evidence that relatively speaking, there is virtually no harm and plenty of advantages in a child being a year older than his peers. On the other hand, there is little benefit but all the disadvantages if a child were a year younger than his peers! But on the point of absolute age, a child is probably better off being 6 rather than 4 while entering school.

In this context, it is disturbing to see schools (not crèches) inviting applications for admission of 18- to 36-month-olds.

You might have seen these fliers in the folds of your newspapers. Well, if the only purpose of these schools is to take the kids off the hands of the parents, that is one thing. But that is what crèches were for, one thought. Exactly what would you want to teach an 18-month-old? If you are scratching your head at that, here is news for you. There are also schools coming up for six-month-olds! Well, talk of abdication of parental responsibility in bringing up children!

One thought there was greater need and not less, to reach out to our children! So how do we do it?

13 Reaching out to children

To understand the heart and mind of a person, look not at what he has already achieved, but at what he aspires to.

—Kahlil Gibran

MOST OF US NEVER CONSCIOUSLY REMEMBER THAT WE were kids once. If we did, we would realize the following:

CHILDREN, IN GENERAL, DISLIKE AND DISTRUST AUTHORITY AND DISCIPLINE

For this very reason, in general children do not like schools, for a school, no matter how good, is by definition a disciplinary or a constraining influence. This is not, however, to say that children must not be disciplined or that no authority should be exercised over them. Without these, anybody is bound to grow up wild. Of course, a child must learn to operate within the confining influences of a disciplining institution that a school is. But having said that, we would do well to remember that basically a child's spirit abhors excessive discipline. Therefore, there is no need to be overly concerned over a child's unenthusiastic attitude to school. It is not uncommon for parents to get into a flap when their child occasionally shows a reluctance to go to school or feigns illness to escape school. We forget, as George Bernard Shaw puts it, 'What we want is to see the child in pursuit of knowledge, and not knowledge in pursuit of the child.' It is more important for a child to develop a wish to learn than be taught. Expecting every child to take to school enthusiastically is unnatural.

This is also a reason why schools must avoid not only corporal punishment, which is banned, at least in theory, but also other kinds of insults and taunts in lieu of corporal punishment, which can have the same effect. It is heartening to note from press reports that educational regulators in the country are looking at bringing even mental torture or harassment of students by teachers under the definition of corporal punishment.

Unfortunately, there remains a gap between what the laws of our land mandate and what we find in reality. Reporting on various forms of torture of children in schools and hostels in Tamil Nadu, the *Deccan Herald* (20 August 2009) quotes a February 2008 report of the National Commission for Protection of Child Rights, stating '...at least 10 schoolchildren had committed suicide after being subjected to various forms of corporal punishment...' We keep seeing scores of similar news items every other day in the media where schools have meted out serious corporal punishment to children to the point of causing serious physical and psychological damage, if not pushing them to their death.

Schools must realize that as sure as Monday follows Sunday, any punishment reinforces a child's aversion to school.

Plato urges us not to 'train children to learning by force and harshness, but direct them to it by what amuses their minds, so that you may be better able to discover with accuracy the peculiar bent of the genius of each'. Perhaps parents need to work more closely with schools to steer them closer to Plato's idea of schooling.

What is more, corporal or other punishment conveys to the child that there are situations where it is all right to slap, beat, smack, punch, assault, insult or be otherwise offensive towards others. It also places a child very directly in line of risk of physical (and not infrequently, mental) injury. What is worse, corporal punishment may result in the child learning how to avoid getting caught rather than changing his behaviour.

'Spare the rod and spoil the child' may be a received wisdom. But action on the adage, particularly by non-parents, teachers in particular included, is decidedly fraught with risk in shaping a child's personality. For that matter, even parents needn't take the adage too seriously. The context of adages must evolve and change as societal values and research on the subject evolve and change. After all we have an adage that tells us 'Many hands make light work'. So should that justify three men to an electric lawnmower that we often see in our country?

CHILDREN, AS A RULE, PREFER GAMES, PLAY AND HANDS-ON TASKS OVER STUDIES, AND WHAT IS MORE, THEY PARTICULARLY DISLIKE EXCESSIVE WORDS

Understanding this fact should motivate parents and teachers alike to make learning fun. Almost every adult has his favourite schoolteacher, who came closest to his ideals. Almost invariably this teacher's classes were fun to sit through. He or she made you do things – made you use your hands, made you want to learn by making you collect leaves from your neighbourhood for your botany homework rather than make you remember fearsome Latin names. For these teachers, you were willing to stretch yourself that extra bit lest he or she be disappointed in you. Almost none of these teachers ever directly forced learning upon you. Thus the onus of making children want to learn is upon teachers and parents and not so much on the students. With children, learning is always easier and more fun if they are made to do things rather than only read. However we often ignore this fact since it is convenient to do so. This is an additional reason why schools must turn to pedagogies which are more active and participative than passive, which are more outdoor-oriented than indoor-oriented, and which are more understanding based than rote-based.

Mahatma Gandhi makes a telling observation in this context, saying, 'Our education has got to be revolutionized. The brain must be educated through the hand. If I were a poet, I could write poetry on the possibilities of the five fingers. Why should you think that the mind is everything and the hands and feet nothing? Those who do not train their hands, who go through the ordinary rut of education, lack "music" in their life. All their faculties are not trained. Mere book knowledge does not interest the child so as to hold his attention fully. The brain gets weary of mere words, and the child's mind begins to wander. Further, he says, 'An education which does not teach us to discriminate between good and bad, to assimilate the one and eschew the other is a misnomer.'[1]

CHILDREN TYPICALLY HAVE A DEEP FEAR AND DISLIKE OF EXAMINATIONS, SINCE EXAMINATIONS EVALUATE THEM, AND A CHILD HAS AN INBUILT FEAR OF FAILURE

As a matter of fact, almost all of us have a fear of being evaluated and children are no exception. Intrinsically, examinations bring fear, anxiety and nervousness in their wake. This is all the more so when the three-hour examination system is more memory-driven than understanding-driven. Examinations cause anxiety also because examinations are a lonesome enterprise which goes against the spirit of collectivity, and children, and for that matter most human beings, are intrinsically gregarious. As my good friend, Manish Sabharwal, chairman of Team Lease, points out, what is called teamwork in informal groups is often called by a different name in formal settings like schools – cheating! Our education hardly provides for teamwork and cooperative methods of working and thus does not prepare the students for real life. Of course I am not necessarily advocating that your kid resort to *teamwork* or *cooperation* in examinations (but then again, why not group assignments, which children

---

[1]   M.K. Gandhi, Discussion with Teacher Trainees, *Harijan*, 18 February 1939, from 'The Collected Works of Mahatma Gandhi,' Navajivan Press (1960), Ahmedabad, Vol. 68, pp. 372-73.

may find a lot more fun?); I am merely trying to draw your attention to the power of informal interactions for children in their formative years.

Open-book examinations or examinations calling for a collective work environment are more difficult or challenging to design, of course. And we adults, take the easy route out and expect the child to take the brunt of our laziness.

CHILDREN MOSTLY LIVE IN THE PRESENT. TRYING TO PUSH THEM HARD FOR A BETTER FUTURE GOES AGAINST THE GRAIN OF CHILDHOOD

Any philosopher would advise us to live in the present. The past is history; the future unknown; and what we have here and now is the present; so enjoy it. That's what we are told as adults. And we forget that children in fact are the living practitioners of this basic philosophy. And yet, rather than let them enjoy their childhood in the present, we build enormous pressures of competitiveness in them to cope with a future which they can barely comprehend. Not surprisingly, we frequently drive them towards stress, strains and occasionally even extreme steps as Page 5 of any newspaper would tell you.

Again, as adults we are exhorted to nurture the 'child' in us! And yet in a real child, we do everything to fast-forward the child into adulthood with grown-up values of cut-throat competition, worrying about the future, coping with stress, ulcers and what have you. We forget that while adulthood is very long, childhood is short. By not allowing a child to be a child, we prevent him from growing into a normal human being. We forget that the sole purpose of the creation of humans could hardly have been to succeed in an entrance exam at 17 or 18. Considering that the numbers who make it into such Ivy League institutions may be barely one per cent of the applicants, one wonders what the remaining 99 per cent children get out of their high-pressure grind!

CHILDREN ARE CURIOUS ABOUT A WIDE RANGE OF THINGS, SO EXPECTING THEM TO CONCENTRATE ON A NARROW RANGE OF ACTIVITIES AS IN FORMAL SCHOOLING OR FORCING THEM INTO REGIMENTED EXTRA-CURRICULAR ACTIVITIES GOES AGAINST THE GRAIN OF CHILDHOOD

It is in childhood that we are most curious. It is in our childhood that we are likely to be interested in a number of pursuits, even if many or most of them are fleeting. This is perhaps nature's way of ensuring that the child explores the world. This then is the exploration phase, when a child is figuring out the world and his relationship to it. By the extreme focus on performance in a narrow range of activities, we take away this opportunity for exploration from children, thus stunting their overall development. We may be having a 'high-performance kid' at the head of the pack, but we are taking away a lot from such a child in terms of the child's ability to cope with life.

EXCESSIVE DISCIPLINE STUNTS A CHILD'S IMAGINATION AND MENTAL GROWTH

Unfortunately, most schools and parents subject their children to excessive discipline and try to fit their lives into straitjackets. For instance, the homework overload, overemphasis on examinations, and pressure on structured and competitive sports all go towards regulating their lives so narrowly that the mind-numbing discipline becomes antithetic to the growth of dreams and imagination of the children.

True, today in most schools corporal punishment has been done away with or has come down substantially. Similarly, most educated parents may have learnt to spare the rod and yet not spoil the child. And yet, an average child's life today remains excessively regulated with undue rigidity in the educational system with its extreme pressure for results, excessive homework, too many tuitions and a host of other structured activities. This has created an environment for children where there is no time for informal play by themselves or with the peer group outside school time. The resulting atmosphere ensures a level of stress of the kind that can break down adults, leave alone children.

A HIGHLY FOCUSED CHILD IS A RARITY AND OFTEN LESS INTERESTING AS AN INDIVIDUAL

I said earlier that a child is intrinsically curious and his mind is like a fluttering butterfly. It is precisely this attribute that makes children lovable and fresh. It is when the stresses and strains of adulthood begin to catch up that this curiosity gives way to cynicism and the dynamic unrest to lethargy. And adults who retain this curiosity and dynamism longer in life almost invariably turn out to be by far the more interesting and accomplished individuals. Why then do we strive so hard to get rid of this spontaneity of curiosity and vigour from children by driving them inexorably towards a narrow goal of short-term performance? With our parenting geared to sprint coaching, aren't we taking away from a child the very attributes which when present even in an adult make him so much more likeable?

INDIRECT INFLUENCES ARE MORE LIKELY TO WORK ON CHILDREN THAN DIRECT ONES

It is widely said and is probably true that most parents try to live their unfulfilled dreams through their children. We would like our children to be the best in everything. We would want them to achieve all that is achievable! But we often forget that if we want our children to internalize the value of hard work, as parents we must be hard-working. If we want them to grow into individuals with strong ethical values, we cannot be bribing that corner policeman for a traffic violation. If we want our children to be well-read, we must be book lovers first. The question is whether you are yourself hard-working, or a person of strong values or deep down a book lover and so forth, or is it that you are trying to get your child to do what you don't? If your child sees you working hard, or practising a strong value system, or learning, he or she is more likely to emulate you. Such implicit influences are more likely to work than pressurizing them into something because you want to live your life through them.

PUTTING DOWN CHILDREN SEVERELY FOR THEIR FAILURES RARELY WORKS IN THE DESIRED DIRECTION

Constant comparison with other children is hardly likely to galvanize your child into higher performance. For one, most children are not intrinsically competitive. They are capable of finding a hundred different things to enjoy and excel in, if only they are left to their own devices. Competition of the kind we adults practise is thrust upon them by us. Comparing them with other children and thus putting them down can frequently lead to lower self-esteem in the child. This is not to say that good examples of other kids should always be a strict 'no-no'; what we are talking about is the obsessive comparison of some parents to get their child to 'keep up with the Joneses' children'.

CHILDREN AREN'T AFRAID OF WORKING HARD

It is not my case, lest I be misunderstood, that children should not work hard. The fact is, children are fresher at the end of the day than most adults are at the beginning of the day. School-going children almost never take a siesta. Often it is a tough task to get them to bed (of course, getting them out of it may be equally tough!). It is not as if children do not like to work hard. If they show great reluctance to complete their homework or study their textbooks, it may be more because these tasks are often so boring. Give a child something that he is interested in and then watch him work! How do you think a lot of children seem to know virtually everything about different models of cars, aeroplanes or dinosaurs? Clearly then, it is far more important to let children follow their passion and areas of interest and channel them in tandem with their formal education rather than blindly goad them on to perform in school.

THE POWER OF VALUES

That the value system which we instil in the minds of children shapes their destiny far more than the schools they go to or the rank they obtain in an examination is highlighted by the story of Ela Bhatt's life.

Ela R. Bhatt came from an enlightened middle-class family in Surat. Her father had a successful law practice, while her mother was active in women's issues. Ela Bhatt went to a local school, Sarvajanik Girls High School, and a local college, M.T.B. College, in Surat to acquire a bachelor's degree in Arts – all in Gujarati medium. She spent another two years at Sir L. A. Shah Law College in Ahmedabad for a law degree.

Ela never topped her school or the college. She might have been in the top 10 percentile, but was never unduly pushed into driving herself very hard. Her father would typically buy a variety of books during the summer vacations and expect her to read them to improve her language skills, which she largely did. Her overall value system was shaped not only by her highly principled father, but the entire nationalistic climate of the time. She was growing up in an India which was all set to break the shackles of British rule. Gandhi was a household name, his teachings the religion of the day, and his life, an example to be emulated. Ela, even as a child, seems to have had a highly developed sense of fairness, as well as being highly sensitive to any form of exploitation of the underprivileged.

Her mother's deep involvement in the women's movement seems to have raised her hackles against the exploitation of women, who she saw were contributing more than their fair share to the economy of the country. But just because they weren't paid for their 'services' and they were not organized in any manner, they seemed to be easy prey for all sorts of exploitation at the hands of the entire organized system. For example, even as a youngster, Ela was sensitive to the fact that while women did most of the agricultural work in the villages, apart from running the households, they did not qualify for any loans from the banking system.

It is awareness of inequities such as these which probably came through her parents' work that shaped Ela's perspective and future. Given her nature, she had to stand up for the underdog. A young Ela saw social work as her calling in order that she could work closely with communities. She contemplated a Masters in Social Works as her first option after her BA. But for this, she would have to move to a city like Bombay, where, in those days, it was not easy for a single girl student to find a suitable hostel. Thus, as the second option she chose to pursue a legal education, which she figured would enable her to fight the exploitation of women through an alternative route.

It is easy to see that her choice of career was neither the first choice, nor a conventional one and not an easy one either, particularly given the times. Nor is the career path typical of the sprinting type. Her 'starts' do not seem to have been great. The India of the early 1950s hardly seems to have been most conducive to a woman lawyer. But that's where the conviction of childhood values takes precedence over a lucrative career.

After her law degree, Ela joined government service in the Textile Labour Association in Ahmedabad, where in due course she headed the Association's Women's Wing. During this stint, she realized that while thousands of women related to textile workers worked hard to supplement the family income, the state laws protected only the industrial workers and never the self-employed women. She took it upon herself to organize these women, and thus SEWA (Self Employed Women's Association) was born.

From here, it was a matter of time before – through her extraordinary commitment, dedication and hard work – SEWA would grow to be the largest organization of its kind for poor working women in the subcontinent. In due course, Ela would found the Women's World Banking, SEWA Cooperative Bank, and preside over a number of other institutions. In 2007, Ela became a founder member of 'The Elders' – along with the likes of Nelson Mandela and Bishop Desmond Tutu, to tackle some of the most challenging problems of the world.

Her life's work would earn her a Ramon Magsaysay award, honorary doctorates from Harvard and Yale, a Padma Bhushan, membership of the Planning Commission, a Rajya Sabha membership and other recognition. But these milestones just happened as she ran the marathon in pursuit of her mission – to help poor women save themselves from exploitation. None of these marked the destination of a sprint.

14 THE LAST WORD

ONE MUST TAKE A LONG-TERM VIEW OF LIFE WHETHER one is a child, a parent, or a professional – that has been the burden of my thesis all along. Sprint may teach you how to buy; marathon will teach you how to build. Sprint may motivate you to take; marathon will teach you to give. Sprint may teach you how to elbow ahead; marathon allows you to lend a helping hand. Sprint may be about how to win; marathon is probably also about how to lose. Sprint may be driven by a desire to be ahead of others; marathon is about being ahead of oneself. Sprint may make you rich; marathon will make you a person of substance.

It also needs to be said that achievement could mean different things to sprinters vis-à-vis marathoners. Achievement in sprint is about winning – as in the position reached or the money made, or fame achieved – typically a life led for oneself. In a marathon it may be more about completing the course itself – as in a life well led, a balance well achieved, time spent on things one found enjoyable or meaningful or with people one loved – probably a life that was inclusive of others.

Marathon precludes none. V. Mani, Subash Bose, T. Raja, Mahantesh G. Kivadasannar, and many others quoted earlier were hardly great achievers to start with. Most of them did not even have a semblance of a good start in life. As a matter of fact, many of them had a really bad start. And yet, all of them have been achievers in every sense of the word, because all of them were obsessed in some way, sooner or later in life – but obsessed they were. What one needs to be a success in life is obsession, sooner or even later in life – not so much a good start. The obsession may be the best start required alongside an upbringing that does not douse that obsession by stereotypical ideas of achievement.

Our conventional wisdom of scrambling for a good start in life; imagining the career as failed just because one didn't get that initial flying start or that one promotion; pushing our children beyond endurance to excel; conditioning them into cracking prized entrance examinations to be called achievers, is flawed. In reality, one can redefine one's life anytime – the earlier, the better – for ourselves and our children.

Index

academic performance, 1–4,
    23–24, 26, 40, 41, 51, 80,
    94, 142, 153
    evaluation system, 5, 116
    and knowledge, 75
    short-term, 155
accomplishment, 60
Adelaide University, 54
adversity, 80
All India Council for Technical
    Education (AICTE), 52
Ambani, Dhirubhai, 47
Animal Planet, 110, 136
Antioch College, 47
Anubhav, 63–65
AP Paper Mills, 128
AP Scooters, 127
aptitude, 73, 102
Augsburg College, 48
authority and discipline,
    147–49

Bacon, Francis, 102

Berea College, 48
Berkshire Hathaway
    Shareholders meeting,
    Omaha (2008), 107
Bhatt, Ela R., 47, 157–60
Binet, Alfred, 50
body language, 6
Bose, Subhash, 63–65, 161
Boston Marathon (1980), 14
Brown University, 47
Buffet, Warren, 46, 53, 107

capitalism and free market, 95
career counseling from parents'
    perspective, 97
career-choosing, 73
caste-ridden biases, 94
Central Board of Secondary
    Education (CBSE), 72
character building, 25
Chattopadhyay, Sarat
    Chandra, 31
cheating, 75, 151

child, child's
   overall development, 39, 45,
      48, 49, 50, 81–82, 86,
      87, 92; through reading
      habit, 104–08
   the parent of man, 21*ff*
   personality, 38, 149
   prodigies, 107, 140–41
   understanding hypothetical
      child, 21–23
childhood passion, 111
City College, New York, 47
classroom teaching, 123
climatic conditions, 12, 26
coaching classes, 38, 45, 49, 74,
   110, 111, 114, 118
coercion and regimen, 101, 113
collectivity, 151
communication skills, 136
comparison with other
   children, 156
competition, 7–8, 15, 29, 38,
   40, 45, 50, 53, 55, 82, 84,
   99, 112, 129, 152, 156
   with others vs competing
      with self, 18
   vs camaraderie, 19–20
competitive exams, 72
competitive sports, 154
competitiveness, 55, 77, 89–90
comprehension and retention,
   97
concentration, lack of, 56

confidence, 39, 75, 105, 141,
   143
cooperation, 29, 50, 55, 105,
   151
corporal punishment, 24,
   148–49, 154
corruption, 41
Council on Trade and
   Industry, 34
creativity, 104, 105, 108
curiosity, 27, 48, 50, 100, 101,
   104, 105, 112, 139, 155
curriculum development, 123
curriculum-linked tests, 104
cynicism, 15

Dartmouth College, 48
Darwin, Charles, 89
Datta, Ashwini (nee
   Nachappa), 78–82
Day, Edward, 74
Dayton, University of (Ohio),
   47
de Castell, Robert, 19
debating, 143
Depauw University, 47
depression, 72, 76
Dhavale, H.S., 73
discipline, 79, 94, 112, 125,
   129
   children dislike and distrust,
      147–49
discovery, 101, 110, 122, 136

Douglas, Norman, 86
Dr Reddy's Laboratories Ltd., 30, 47
Dweck, Carol S., 120–21
Dyer, Wayne, 59

education, education system, 85, 91, 92, 98–100, 102, 105, 114, 123, 135, 141, 154
function and purpose of, 27–28, 100–01
Einstein, Albert, 100, 15, 139
Eliot, T.S., 102
Emerson, Ralph Waldo, 83, 140
emotional maturity, 136
energy vs mental toughness, 13–14
enquiry, spirit of, 122
entrance examinations, 87, 91, 117–18, 162
entrepreneurship, 57–58, 127, 129–30
evaluation process, 117, 123
understanding the fear of, 116–17
examination(s)
fear, 151
open-book, 152
oriented education, 133–34
overemphasis on, 154
system, 26, 72, 84, 105, 116–18, 122, 151

extra-curricular activities, 153

failure, 156
and child's preparedness to face, 119–21
family, 6, 10, 36
bonding, 116, 124, 130
culture and reading, 98, 106–07
and career choosing, 124–30
Fox History, 110
fulfilment, sense of, 62

Gandhi, M.K., 64, 150, 158
Gareau, Jacqueline, 14
Gettysburg College, 47
Gibran, Kahlil, 147
Gill, Mohinder Singh, 79
Gladwell, Malcolm, 47, 143–44
Gopinath, G.R., 47
Goyal, Ashish, 68–70
grammar and sentence formation skills, 125
Grinnell College, 48
group assignments, 122

Hamilton College, 47
hard work, 33, 48, 80, 130, 141, 155, 159
Hazlitt, William, 60
high blood pressure, 75–76
Hilton, Paris, 42

History Channel, 136
hobbies, 109–11
Holy Cross, 47
homework, 1–3, 22, 76, 122,
    150, 154, 157
Hunter College, 47
Hymowitz, Carol, 45

Illinois, University of, 47
imagination, 154
Indian Drugs and
    Pharmaceuticals Ltd.
    (IDPL), 33, 35
inequities, 158
inferiority complex, 92
influences, indirect, 155
Infosys, 46
innovation and
    experimentation, 25, 123,
    135
inquiry. See questioning
intelligence, 101, 117–18
Internet, 2
intrinsic interests, 111
Irvine, Sister Marion, 17, 43
Ivy League institutions, 45–46,
    49–51, 153

Jacobs, 64
jobs and careers, 99–100

Kansas, 54

Karunashraya, 66–67
Kennedy, John F., 145
Kivadasannavar, Mahantesh
    G., 67–68, 161
knowledge, 9, 25, 113, 148,
    150
    and academic performance,
        75, 118
    acquisition, 84–85
    and the application of
        knowledge, 136
    goal of mankind, 101
    and reading, 97, 100–01,
        105, 108
    and schools, 113
Kohn, Alfie, 116
Krishnamurti Foundation, 84,
    101
Krishnamurti, J., 84, 101
kunjis (help books), 114

Lafley, A.G., 46
language and communication
    skills, 97
leadership, 25
learning, 112–13, 115–17,
    149–50
    by doing, 122
    from failures, 124–32
    to learn, 50
    oriented system, 121–23
    play oriented, 122

Lee, R.E. Mark, 101
licence-permit raj, 34, 132

Mackay, Harvey, 58–59
Mahbubani, Kishore, 57
Mandela, Nelson, 159
Mani, V., 62–63, 161
Massachusetts, University of, 48
Mastru, Patnayak, 126
mediocrity, 135
memory, 31–32, 35–36, 44, 83
  and examination, 151
  rote, 137
  short-term, 38, 122
mental
  and emotional make-up, 11
  growth, 154
  health of adolescent girls, 73
  torture, 148
  toughness, 26
Miller, Michelle, 74
mind and body, 14
mindset, 121
Mirza, Sania, 116
moral character, 22, 92
motivation, 25, 43, 86, 91, 100, 126, 131, 149

Nadar, Shiv, 47
Murthy, N.R. Narayana, 46, 48, 57, 93–95
National Geographic, 110, 136

Nebraska, University of, 48
New Ark Mission, 65–66
non-sports activities, 143
Notre Dame, University of, 47
Nurmi, Paavo, 14
nursery admissions, 91

obedience, 105
objective-type examinations, 45
Ohio Wesleyan University, 48
Olympics, 14
organization building, 25
originality, 123
Otellini, Paul, 46
over-parenting, 56, 72, 96, 132
over-schooling, 56, 86
over-tutoring, 56

parental pressures, 54, 71–77, 80–81, 111
parental role model, 107
parenting style, 79–80, 115–16, 135
parents'
  ego, 39
  unfulfilled desires and ambitions, 73–74
  values, effect on children, 77–79
Patel, Karsanbhai, 47
Patton, S., 14
Pausch, Randy, 121
Pavlova, Anna, 44, 60

pedagogical philosophy, 86

performance. *See* academic
performance

personality, 117
disorders, 54

physical attributes, 144

physiology and psychology, 15

Plato, 149

Pope, Denise, 75

positive reinforcements, 79

questioning, 100, 133, 139

Raja, T., 65–66, 161

Ramadorai, S., 47

Ramanujam, 107

Rampal, Anita, 113

rankings, 105

Rao, Damiri Venkata, 125

Rao, G. Mallikarjuna, 46, 48,
124–32

Rao, Kishore S., 66

Rao, P.D.K., 42

reading, 96*ff*
habits, 104
and learning, 107, 115
and professionals, 103
and teaching, 102–03

reasoning, 135

Reddy, Kalam Anji, 30–36,
47, 48

right attitude, 37*ff*

Rishi Valley School, Chittoor
District, 84, 85

risk-taking ability, 104

role models, 42, 98, 102, 107

Rollins College (Florida), 48

rote learning, 105, 114, 117

rote memory, 137

rote-based conditioning as
learning, 113

rote-based, 150

Sabharwal, Manish, 151

Samarthan Trust for the
Disabled, 67–68

school
curriculum, 27, 28, 91
government, 122
private, 122

schooling, 107, 139
formal, 153
and mediocrity, 112*ff*
work life and competition,
83*ff*

Scott, Lee, 46

SD College, 141

SD High School, 141

Self Employed Women's
Association (SEWA), 47,
159

self, sense, 121

self-control, 92

self-esteem, 92, 120, 156

self-learning opportunities, 122

sense of success, happiness or

satisfaction, 88–89
SEWA Cooperative Bank, 159
Shankar, Ravi, 40
Shaw, George Bernard, 148
social interaction, 82
social skills, 108
Society's Care for the Indigent (SOCARE), 62–63
socio-economic conditions, 110
Sodhana Charitable Trust, 42
spontaneity, 113
Standard Organics Ltd, 34
State Trading Corporation (STC), 33–34
stimulation, 139
strategic persistence, 15
strength vs stamina, 13
stress, 50, 71, 75–76, 132, 152, 154
Stressed Out Students (SOS), 75
student, development, 84–85
success, 10, 39, 41–44, 60–61, 66, 88–89, 93–94, 120, 129, 162
    academic performance, 93
    business, 89
    meaningful, 26
    standards, 90
suicides among children, 71, 73, 74

Tagore, Rabindranath, 31, 64

Tammeus, William D., 133
teaching-oriented educational system, 121–23
Team Lease, 151
team spirit, teamwork, 25, 29, 50, 113, 151
technological proficiency, 84
Tendulkar, Sachin, 40
Texas, University of, 47
textbooks
    and knowledge, 102, 117, 157
    preoccupation with, 27
Textile Labour Association, 159
thinking kid, 137
Tillerson, Rex, 46
Toronto, University of, 48
Travel and Living, 110
Trump, Donald, 61
tuitions, 7, 113. *See also* coaching
Tutu, Bishop Desmond, 159

uncertainty element, 17
under-parenting, 132
unhappiness at failure, 55, 56
Uniform Civil Code, 134
Union College (Kentucky), 47
Updike, John, 112
US Olympic Marathon trials (1984), 17, 43
Usha, P.T., 79, 80

relative or absolute, 88

Valley School, Bangalore, 84
value system, 149, 155, 157
Viswanathan, Anand, 40
Vivekananda, Swami, 101
vocabulary, 108
vocational skills, 122

Wharton School of
   Management, 69
Williams, Rowan, 75
Winfrey, Oprah, 8
winning vs running, 17
Wolfe, Thomas, 41

Washington, University of, 47
well-being, 108
   mental, 109

Yeats, William Butler, 114

Zatopek, Emil, 10